Quick & Easy
CASSEROLES

FAVORITE ALL TIME RECIPES is a trademark of Publications International, Ltd.

Copyright ©1989 Durkee-French Foods, A Division of Reckitt & Colman Inc.

Tested recipes from the kitchens of Durkee-French Foods.

This edition published by:
Publications International, Ltd.
7373 N. Cicero Ave.
Lincolnwood, IL 60646

Manufactured in U.S.A.

8   7   6   5   4   3   2   1

ISBN: 0-7853-0063-5

Pictured on the front cover: Mustard Chicken & Vegetables *(page 10)*.

Pictured on the back cover *(clockwise from top left)*: Mini Meat Loaves & Vegetables *(page 48)*; Original Green Bean Casserole and Swiss Vegetable Medley *(page 84)*; Hearty Chicken Bake *(page 15)*.

PUBLICATIONS INTERNATIONAL, LTD.

DURKEE—THE SECRET TO GREAT CASSEROLES

This book was designed with you in mind—the busy cook. Casseroles featuring minimum preparation time, make-ahead convenience and no-watch baking are the perfect answer to today's hectic lifestyles. Whether it's a family meal, a special dinner or a potluck supper, you'll find the perfect time-saving main course or side dish. Most are ready to pop into the oven in 15 minutes or less!

In addition to quick and easy preparation, every casserole in this collection has the "special touch" of Durkee French Fried Onions. The crisp crunch, savory onion flavor and golden eye appeal of French Fried Onions turn ordinary dishes into extraordinary delights!

Just what makes Durkee French Fried Onions such a unique product? For 54 years, Durkee French Fried Onions have been made from select prime quality yellow globe onions grown only in New York State. The onions are sliced, coated with a specially formulated wheat flour batter and fried in vegetable oil. After frying, the onions are dried under controlled conditions and vacuum-packed for maximum freshness.

All the recipes in this book were developed by skilled home economists in the Durkee Famous Foods Test Kitchen, were taste tested by consumers, and were retested again and again to ensure success. The "ready-to-bake" times given for the recipes are based on minutes required to assemble the casseroles. They include such preparations as opening cans, peeling and chopping vegetables, and shredding cheese. The times also take into account that some preparations can be done simultaneously, such as preparing a biscuit topping while a mixture is simmering. Preparations *not* calculated into these times include advance cooking of ingredients, such as pasta, rice and bacon, boning chicken, and the thawing of frozen vegetables.

Thawing Frozen Vegetables: Most recipes call for thawed frozen vegetables. It is necessary to thaw the vegetables or baking time and final recipe consistency will be affected. To easily thaw frozen vegetables, place in colander and run under cold water. Or, defrost in microwave oven according to manufacturer's directions. Drain vegetables well. Note: *Do not* thaw frozen potatoes under cold water; thaw according to manufacturer's directions.

Reheating Pasta and Rice: Many recipes specify *hot* cooked pasta or rice. If pasta or rice is made in advance, reheat it before adding to recipes or baking time will be affected. To reheat, place in colander; pour boiling water evenly over pasta or rice and let drain.

Baking Dish Size: It is important to use the dish size specified in the recipe. A different size could affect the recipe's success.

Microwave Cooking: All microwave directions were tested in countertop microwave ovens rated at 600 to 700 watts. Microwave cooking times are approximate due to numerous variables, such as starting temperatures, shape, amount of food, etc. Watch casseroles carefully and adjust cooking times for your specific oven.

FRENCH FRIED ONION TIPS

- One 2.8-ounce can equals 1⅓ cups.
- One 6-ounce can equals approximately 3 cups.
- To enjoy the total French Fried Onion experience of flavor, crunch and eye appeal, mix ½ can with casserole ingredients and use remaining ½ can for final topping.
- When taking a casserole to a potluck dinner or picnic, reserve final ½ can French Fried Onions and sprinkle on casserole just before serving.
- To toast French Fried Onions for later addition to casseroles or for snacking, bake in 350° oven for 1 to 2 minutes or microwave on HIGH 1 minute.

MINUTE-WISE POULTRY

CHICKEN IN FRENCH ONION SAUCE

Ready to bake in just 7 easy minutes

1 package (10 ounces) frozen
  baby carrots, thawed and
  drained or 4 medium
  carrots, cut into strips
  (about 2 cups)
2 cups sliced mushrooms
½ cup thinly sliced celery
1 can (2.8 ounces) Durkee
  French Fried Onions

4 chicken breast halves,
  skinned and boned
½ cup white wine
¾ cup prepared chicken
  bouillon
½ teaspoon garlic salt
½ teaspoon pepper
  Paprika

Preheat oven to 375°. In 8×12-inch baking dish, combine vegetables and ½ *can* French Fried Onions. Arrange chicken breasts on vegetables. In small bowl, combine wine, bouillon, garlic salt and pepper; pour over chicken and vegetables. Sprinkle chicken with paprika. Bake, covered, at 375° for 35 minutes or until chicken is done. Baste chicken with wine sauce and top with remaining onions; bake, uncovered, 3 minutes or until onions are golden brown.   *Makes 4 servings*

MICROWAVE DIRECTIONS: In 8×12-inch microwave-safe dish, combine vegetables and ½ *can* onions. Arrange chicken breasts, skinned side down, along sides of dish. Prepare wine mixture as above, except reduce bouillon to ⅓ cup; pour over chicken and vegetables. Cook, covered, on HIGH 6 minutes. Turn chicken breasts over and sprinkle with paprika. Stir vegetables and rotate dish. Cook, covered, 7 to 9 minutes or until chicken is done. Baste chicken with wine sauce and top with remaining onions; cook, uncovered, 1 minute. Let stand 5 minutes.

CURRIED CHICKEN POT PIE

Ready to bake in just 10 easy minutes

2 cups (10 ounces) cubed
   cooked chicken
1 bag (16 ounces) frozen
   vegetable combination
   (cauliflower, carrots,
   broccoli), thawed and
   drained
1 can (2.8 ounces) Durkee
   French Fried Onions
1 cup (4 ounces) shredded
   Cheddar cheese

1 can (10¾ ounces) condensed
   cream of chicken soup
⅔ cup milk
½ teaspoon seasoned salt
¼ teaspoon curry powder
1 (9-inch) folded refrigerated
   unbaked pie crust

Preheat oven to 400°. In 9-inch pie plate, combine chicken, vegetables, *½ can* French Fried Onions and *½ cup* cheese. In small bowl, combine soup, milk and seasonings; pour over chicken mixture and stir to combine. Place pie crust over chicken mixture; seal edges and cut 4 steam vents. Bake, uncovered, at 400° for 40 minutes or until crust is golden brown. Top with remaining cheese and onions; bake, uncovered, 1 to 3 minutes or until onions are golden brown.

Makes 4 to 6 servings

LATTICE-TOP CHICKEN

Ready to bake in just 12 easy minutes

1 can (10¾ ounces) condensed
   cream of potato soup
1¼ cups milk
½ teaspoon seasoned
   salt
1½ cups (7 ounces) cubed cooked
   chicken
1 bag (16 ounces) frozen
   vegetable combination
   (broccoli, carrots,
   cauliflower), thawed and
   drained

1 cup (4 ounces) shredded
   Cheddar cheese
1 can (2.8 ounces) Durkee
   French Fried Onions
1 cup biscuit baking mix*
¼ cup milk
1 egg, slightly beaten

*1 package (4 ounces) refrigerated crescent rolls may be substituted for baking mix, ¼ cup milk and egg. Separate dough into 2 rectangles; press together perforated cuts. Cut each rectangle lengthwise into 3 strips. Arrange strips on hot chicken mixture to form lattice. Top as directed. Bake, uncovered, at 375° for 15 to 20 minutes or until lattice is golden brown.

(continued)

Lattice-Top Chicken

Preheat oven to 375°. In large bowl, combine soup, 1¼ cups milk, seasoned salt, chicken, vegetables, ½ *cup* cheese and ½ *can* French Fried Onions. Pour into 8×12-inch baking dish. Bake, covered, at 375° for 15 minutes. Meanwhile, in small bowl, combine baking mix, ¼ cup milk and egg to form soft dough. Stir casserole and spoon dough over hot chicken mixture to form lattice design. Bake, uncovered, 20 to 25 minutes or until lattice is golden brown. Top lattice with remaining cheese and onions; bake, uncovered, 3 minutes or until onions are golden brown.

Makes 4 to 6 servings

MICROWAVE DIRECTIONS: Prepare chicken mixture as above; pour into 8×12-inch microwave-safe dish. Cook, covered, on HIGH 10 minutes or until heated through. Stir chicken mixture halfway through cooking time. Prepare biscuit dough and spoon over casserole as above. Cook, uncovered, 7 to 9 minutes or until lattice is done. Rotate dish halfway through cooking time. Top lattice with remaining cheese and onions; cook, uncovered, 1 minute or until cheese melts. Let stand 5 minutes.

CHILI-CHICKEN SOMBREROS

Ready to bake in just 10 easy minutes

2½ cups (13 ounces) cubed
    cooked chicken
1 can (4 ounces) chopped green
    chilies, drained
1½ cups (6 ounces) shredded
    sharp Cheddar cheese
1 medium tomato, chopped
1 can (10¾ ounces) condensed
    cream of chicken soup
½ cup milk

½ teaspoon Durkee RedHot®
    Cayenne Pepper Sauce
    (optional)
¾ cup biscuit baking mix
⅔ cup cornmeal
⅔ cup milk
1 can (2.8 ounces) Durkee
    French Fried Onions
Chili powder

Preheat oven to 375°. In greased 8×12-inch baking dish, layer chicken, chilies, *1 cup* cheese and the tomato. In small bowl, combine soup, ½ cup milk and cayenne pepper sauce; pour evenly over chicken mixture. Bake, covered, at 375° for 20 minutes. Meanwhile, in medium bowl, combine baking mix, cornmeal, ⅔ cup milk and ½ *can* French Fried Onions; beat vigorously 30 seconds. Spoon biscuit dough in 8 mounds over top of casserole. Sprinkle biscuits with chili powder. Bake, uncovered, 20 minutes or until biscuits are light brown. Top biscuits with remaining cheese and onions; bake, uncovered, 3 minutes or until onions are golden brown. *Makes 6 to 8 servings*

CREAMY TURKEY & BROCCOLI

Ready to bake in just 18 easy minutes

1 package (6 ounces) stuffing
    mix,* plus ingredients to
    prepare mix
1 can (2.8 ounces) Durkee
    French Fried Onions
1 package (10 ounces) frozen
    broccoli spears, thawed and
    drained

1 package (about 1⅛ ounces)
    cheese sauce mix
1¼ cups milk
½ cup sour cream
2 cups (10 ounces) cubed
    cooked turkey or chicken

*3 cups leftover stuffing may be substituted for stuffing mix. If stuffing is dry, stir in water, 1 tablespoon at a time, until moist but not wet.

Preheat oven to 350°. In medium saucepan, prepare stuffing mix according to package directions; stir in ½ *can* French Fried Onions. Spread stuffing over bottom of greased 9-inch round baking dish. Arrange broccoli spears over stuffing with flowerets around edge of

(continued)

Creamy Turkey & Broccoli

dish. In medium saucepan, prepare cheese sauce mix according to package directions using 1¼ cups milk. Remove from heat; stir in sour cream and turkey. Pour turkey mixture over broccoli *stalks*. Bake, covered, at 350° for 30 minutes or until heated through. Sprinkle remaining onions over turkey; bake, uncovered, 5 minutes or until onions are golden brown. *Makes 4 to 6 servings*

MICROWAVE DIRECTIONS: In 9-inch round microwave-safe dish, prepare stuffing mix according to package microwave directions; stir in ½ *can* onions. Arrange stuffing and broccoli spears in dish as above; set aside. In medium microwave-safe bowl, prepare cheese sauce mix according to package microwave directions using 1¼ cups milk. Add turkey and cook, covered, 5 to 6 minutes, stirring turkey halfway through cooking time. Stir in sour cream. Pour turkey mixture over broccoli *stalks*. Cook, covered, 8 to 10 minutes or until heated through. Rotate dish halfway through cooking time. Top turkey with remaining onions; cook, uncovered, 1 minute. Let stand 5 minutes.

MUSTARD CHICKEN & VEGETABLES

Ready to bake in just 15 easy minutes

2 cups (8 ounces) fusilli or rotini, cooked in unsalted water and drained
¼ cup Dijon-style or prepared mustard
¼ cup vegetable oil
1 tablespoon red wine vinegar
½ teaspoon dried oregano, crumbled
¼ teaspoon pepper
¼ teaspoon salt

2 pounds chicken pieces, fat trimmed
1 can (10¾ ounces) condensed cream of chicken soup
½ cup milk
1 cup *each* zucchini and yellow squash, cut into 1-inch chunks
1 can (2.8 ounces) Durkee French Fried Onions
1 medium tomato, cut into wedges

Preheat oven to 375°. In large bowl, combine mustard, oil, vinegar and seasonings; mix well. Toss chicken in mustard sauce until coated. Reserve remaining mustard sauce. Arrange chicken in 9 × 13-inch baking dish. Bake, uncovered, at 375° for 30 minutes. Stir soup, milk, hot pasta, squash and ½ *can* French Fried Onions into remaining mustard sauce. Spoon pasta mixture into baking dish, placing it under and around chicken. Bake, uncovered, 15 to 20 minutes or until chicken is done. Top pasta mixture with tomato wedges and top chicken with remaining onions; bake, uncovered, 3 minutes or until onions are golden brown.   *Makes 4 to 6 servings*

MICROWAVE DIRECTIONS: Prepare mustard sauce as above; add chicken and toss until coated. Reserve remaining mustard sauce. In 8 × 12-inch microwave-safe dish, arrange chicken with meatiest parts toward edges of dish. Cook, uncovered, on HIGH 10 minutes. Rearrange chicken. Prepare pasta mixture and add to chicken as above. Cook, uncovered, 15 to 17 minutes or until chicken and vegetables are done. Stir vegetables and pasta and rotate dish halfway through cooking time. Top with tomato wedges and remaining onions as above; cook, uncovered, 1 minute. Let stand 5 minutes.

TURKEY CORDON BLEU

Ready to bake in just 10 easy minutes

1 pound uncooked turkey
   breast slices
1 can (2.8 ounces) Durkee
   French Fried Onions
4 slices (1 ounce *each*) Swiss
   cheese, cut into halves
2 slices (1 ounces *each*) cooked
   turkey ham or ham, cut
   into halves

1 can (10¾ ounces) condensed
   cream of chicken soup
¼ cup milk
1 medium tomato, cut into
   4 slices

Preheat oven to 375°. In 7×11-inch baking dish, arrange turkey slices in 4 equal stacks. Top each stack with ¼ *cup* French Fried Onions, ½ *slice* cheese and ½ *slice* ham. In small bowl, combine soup and milk; pour over turkey stacks. Bake, covered, at 375° for 30 minutes or until turkey is done. Top stacks with remaining cheese slices, the tomato slices and remaining onions. Bake, uncovered, 3 minutes or until onions are golden brown. Serve over rice, noodles or toast.   *Makes 4 servings*

MICROWAVE DIRECTIONS: In 7×11-inch microwave-safe dish, assemble turkey stacks as above. Prepare soup mixture as above; pour over turkey stacks. Cook, covered, on HIGH 10 to 12 minutes or until turkey is done. Rotate dish halfway through cooking time. Top stacks with remaining cheese slices, the tomato slices and remaining onions; cook, uncovered, 1 minute or until cheese melts. Let stand 5 minutes.

ZESTY CHICKEN & RICE

Ready to bake in just 7 easy minutes

⅔ cup uncooked regular rice
1 can (2.8 ounces) Durkee
   French Fried Onions
½ teaspoon Italian seasoning
1¾ cups prepared chicken
   bouillon
4 chicken breast halves, fat
   trimmed, skinned
   if desired

⅓ cup bottled Italian salad
   dressing
1 bag (16 ounces) frozen
   vegetable combination
   (broccoli, carrots, water
   chestnuts, red pepper)

Preheat oven to 400°. In 9×13-inch baking dish, combine uncooked rice, ½ *can* French Fried Onions and the Italian seasoning. Pour bouillon over rice mixture. Arrange chicken breasts on top; pour

(continued)

Zesty Chicken & Rice

salad dressing over chicken. Bake, covered, at 400° for 30 minutes. Place vegetables around chicken, covering rice. Bake, uncovered, 20 to 25 minutes or until chicken and rice are done. Top chicken with remaining onions; bake, uncovered, 1 to 3 minutes or until onions are golden brown. *Makes 4 servings*

MICROWAVE DIRECTIONS: Reduce bouillon to 1¼ cups. In 8×12-inch microwave-safe dish, combine uncooked rice and bouillon. Cook, covered, on HIGH 5 minutes, stirring rice halfway through cooking time. Stir in vegetables, *½ can* onions and Italian seasoning. Arrange chicken over vegetable mixture with meatiest parts toward edges of dish. Pour salad dressing over chicken. Cook, covered, on MEDIUM (50-60%) 15 to 17 minutes or until chicken and rice are done. Rearrange chicken and rotate dish halfway through cooking time. Top chicken with remaining onions; cook, uncovered, on HIGH 1 minute. Let stand 5 minutes.

CALIFORNIA-STYLE CHICKEN

Ready to bake in just 15 easy minutes

1 can (15 ounces) tomato
sauce
3 tablespoons red wine vinegar
½ teaspoon dried basil,
crumbled
¼ teaspoon garlic powder
12 small red potatoes, thinly
sliced (about 3 cups)

1 can (2.8 ounces) Durkee
French Fried Onions
2½ pounds chicken pieces, fat
trimmed, skinned if desired
1 package (10 ounces) frozen
whole green beans, thawed
and drained

Preheat oven to 375°. In small bowl, combine tomato sauce, vinegar
and seasonings. Spread *½ cup* tomato mixture in bottom of 9×13-
inch baking dish; top with potatoes and *½ can* French Fried Onions.
Arrange chicken over potatoes and onions. Spoon *1 cup* tomato
mixture over chicken and potatoes. Bake, covered, at 375° for 35
minutes. Stir green beans into potatoes. Spoon remaining tomato
mixture over chicken. Bake, covered, 10 to 15 minutes or until
chicken and beans are done. Top chicken with remaining onions;
bake, uncovered, 3 minutes or until onions are golden brown.

Makes 4 to 6 servings

CHICKEN-MAC CASSEROLE

Ready to bake in just 20 easy minutes

1½ cups elbow macaroni, cooked
in unsalted water and
drained
6 slices bacon, fried crisp and
crumbled
2 cups (10 ounces) cubed
cooked chicken
1 can (2.8 ounces) Durkee
French Fried Onions

1 can (10¾ ounces) condensed
cream of mushroom soup
1 cup sour cream
1 package (10 ounces) frozen
chopped spinach, thawed
and well drained
⅛ teaspoon garlic powder
1½ cups (6 ounces) shredded
Cheddar cheese

Preheat oven to 375°. Return hot macaroni to saucepan; stir in
bacon, chicken and *½ can* French Fried Onions. In medium bowl,
combine soup, sour cream, spinach, garlic powder and *1 cup*
Cheddar cheese. Spoon *half* the macaroni mixture into greased
8×12-inch baking dish; cover with *half* the spinach mixture. Repeat
layers. Bake, covered, at 375° for 30 minutes or until heated
through. Top with remaining cheese and onions. Bake, uncovered,
3 minutes or until onions are golden brown.

Makes 6 to 8 servings

HEARTY CHICKEN BAKE

Ready to bake in just 12 easy minutes

3 cups hot mashed potatoes
1 cup (4 ounces) shredded
  Cheddar cheese
1 can (2.8 ounces) Durkee
  French Fried Onions
1½ cups (7 ounces) cubed cooked
  chicken
1 package (10 ounces) frozen
  mixed vegetables, thawed
  and drained

1 can (10¾ ounces) condensed
  cream of chicken soup
¼ cup milk
½ teaspoon ground mustard
¼ teaspoon garlic powder
¼ teaspoon pepper

Preheat oven to 375°. In medium bowl, combine mashed potatoes, ½ *cup* cheese and ½ *can* French Fried Onions; mix thoroughly. Spoon potato mixture into greased 1½-quart casserole. Using back of spoon, spread potatoes across bottom and up sides of dish to form a shell. In large bowl, combine chicken, mixed vegetables, soup, milk and seasonings; pour into potato shell. Bake, uncovered, at 375° for 30 minutes or until heated through. Top with remaining cheese and onions; bake, uncovered, 3 minutes or until onions are golden brown. Let stand 5 minutes before serving.

Makes 4 to 6 servings

Hearty Chicken Bake

EASY ONION-STUFFED TURKEY ROLLS

Ready to bake in just 15 easy minutes

1¼ cups water
¼ cup butter or margarine
3½ cups seasoned stuffing crumbs*
1 can (2.8 ounces) Durkee French Fried Onions

8 thin slices deli turkey breast (about 10 ounces)
1 can (10¾ ounces) condensed cream of chicken soup
½ cup milk
1 package (10 ounces) frozen peas, thawed and drained

Preheat oven to 350°. In medium saucepan, heat water and butter; stir until butter melts. Remove from heat. Stir in seasoned stuffing crumbs and ½ *can* French Fried Onions. Divide stuffing equally between turkey slices; spread across 1 end of each slice. Roll up turkey slices jelly-roll style and place, seam-side down, in 2 rows of 4 in 8×12-inch baking dish. In medium bowl, combine soup, milk and peas; spoon over turkey rolls. Bake, covered, at 350° for 30 minutes or until heated through. Top turkey rolls with remaining onions; bake, uncovered, 5 minutes or until onions are golden brown.
Makes 4 servings

*3 cups leftover stuffing may be substituted for butter, water and stuffing crumbs. If stuffing is dry, stir in water, 1 tablespoon at a time, until moist but not wet.

CHICKEN DIVAN

Ready to bake in just 10 easy minutes

1½ cups cooked unsalted regular rice (½ cup uncooked)
1 package (10 ounces) frozen broccoli spears, thawed and drained
1 can (2.8 ounces) Durkee French Fried Onions
1 can (10¾ ounces) condensed cream of chicken soup

½ cup sour cream
½ cup (2 ounces) shredded Cheddar cheese
1 teaspoon paprika
¼ teaspoon curry powder (optional)
1 cup (5 ounces) cubed cooked chicken

Preheat oven to 350°. In 10-inch pie plate, arrange broccoli spears with flowerets around edge of dish. (May be necessary to halve stalks to obtain enough flowerets.) To hot rice in saucepan, add ½ *can* French Fried Onions, the soup, sour cream, cheese, seasonings and chicken; stir well. Spoon chicken mixture evenly over broccoli *stalks*. Bake, covered, at 350° for 30 minutes or until heated through. Top with remaining onions; bake, uncovered, 5 minutes or until onions are golden brown.
Makes 4 servings

Jiffy Chicken 'n Rice

Ready to bake in just 5 easy minutes

1½ cups cooked unsalted regular rice (½ cup uncooked)
1 jar (8 ounces) pasteurized processed cheese spread
¼ cup milk

2 cups (10 ounces) cubed cooked chicken
1 package (10 ounces) frozen peas, thawed and drained
1 can (2.8 ounces) Durkee French Fried Onions

Preheat oven to 375°. To hot rice in saucepan, add cheese spread, milk, chicken, peas and ½ can French Fried Onions; stir well. Spoon into 1½-quart casserole. Bake, covered, at 375° for 25 minutes or until heated through. Top with remaining onions; bake, uncovered, 3 minutes or until onions are golden brown.

Makes 4 to 6 servings

MICROWAVE DIRECTIONS: Prepare rice mixture as above; spoon into 1½-quart microwave-safe casserole. Cook, covered, on HIGH 8 to 10 minutes or until heated through. Stir rice mixture halfway through cooking time. Top with remaining onions; cook, uncovered, 1 minute. Let stand 5 minutes.

Oriental Chicken Medley

Ready to bake in just 7 easy minutes

3 cups cooked unsalted regular rice (1 cup uncooked)
2 cups (10 ounces) cubed cooked chicken
1 medium green pepper, cut into strips
1 can (10¾ ounces) condensed cream of mushroom soup

¾ cup water
2 tablespoons soy sauce
1 tablespoon diced pimiento
¼ teaspoon ground ginger
1 can (2.8 ounces) Durkee French Fried Onions

Preheat oven to 350°. To hot rice in saucepan, add chicken, green pepper, soup, water, soy sauce, pimiento, ginger and ½ can French Fried Onions; stir well. Pour into 2-quart casserole. Bake, uncovered, at 350° for 40 minutes or until heated through. Top with remaining onions; bake, uncovered, 5 minutes or until onions are golden brown.

Makes 4 to 6 servings

MICROWAVE DIRECTIONS: Prepare rice mixture as above; pour into 8×12-inch microwave-safe dish. Cook, covered, on HIGH 10 to 15 minutes or until heated through. Stir casserole halfway through cooking time. Top with remaining onions; cook, uncovered, 1 minute. Let stand 5 minutes.

Homespun Turkey 'n Vegetables

Ready to bake in just 10 easy minutes

1 package (9 ounces) frozen cut green beans, thawed and drained

1 can (14 ounces) sliced carrots, drained

1 can (2.8 ounces) Durkee French Fried Onions

1 can (16 ounces) whole potatoes, drained

1 can (10¾ ounces) condensed cream of celery soup

¼ cup milk

1 tablespoon prepared mustard

¼ teaspoon garlic powder

1 pound uncooked turkey breast slices

Preheat oven to 375°. In 8 × 12-inch baking dish, combine green beans, carrots and ½ *can* French Fried Onions. Slice potatoes into halves; arrange as many halves as will fit, cut-side down, around edges of baking dish. Combine any remaining potatoes with vegetables in dish. In medium bowl, combine soup, milk, mustard and garlic powder; pour *half* the soup mixture over vegetables. Overlap turkey slices on vegetables. Pour remaining soup mixture over turkey and potatoes. Bake, covered, at 375° for 40 minutes or until turkey is done. Top turkey with remaining onions; bake, uncovered, 3 minutes or until onions are golden brown.

Makes 4 servings

Chicken Cazuela

Ready to bake in just 7 easy minutes

8 ounces linguini, broken in half, cooked in unsalted water and drained

1 can (2.8 ounces) Durkee French Fried Onions

2 cups (10 ounces) cubed cooked chicken

1 can (10¾ ounces) condensed cream of mushroom soup

½ cup prepared chicken bouillon

1 can (4 ounces) chopped green chilies, drained

2 tablespoons diced pimiento

1 cup (4 ounces) shredded cheddar cheese

Preheat oven to 350°. In greased 8 × 12-inch baking dish, layer hot linguini, ½ *can* French Fried Onions and the chicken. In small bowl, combine soup, bouillon, chilies and pimiento; pour over chicken. Top with cheese. Bake, covered, at 350° for 30 minutes or until heated through. Top with remaining onions; bake, uncovered, 5 minutes or until onions are golden brown. *Makes 6 to 8 servings*

Homespun Turkey 'n Vegetables

CHICKEN AND RED RICE

Ready to bake in just 5 easy minutes

⅔ cup uncooked regular rice
1 cup chopped green pepper
1 can (2.8 ounces) Durkee
    French Fried Onions
4 chicken breast halves, fat
    trimmed, skinned
    if desired

1 jar (15½ ounces) spaghetti
    sauce with mushrooms
1¼ cups water

Preheat oven to 375°. In 8×12-inch baking dish, combine uncooked rice, green pepper and ½ *can* French Fried Onions. Arrange chicken breasts over rice mixture. In medium bowl, combine spaghetti sauce and water; pour over chicken and rice. Bake, covered, at 375° for 50 minutes or until chicken and rice are done. Top chicken with remaining onions; bake, uncovered, 3 minutes or until onions are golden brown.

Makes 4 servings

MICROWAVE DIRECTIONS: Reduce water to 1 cup. In 8×12-inch microwave-safe dish, combine uncooked rice and water. Cook, covered, on HIGH 10 minutes, stirring rice halfway through cooking time. Stir green pepper and ½ *can* onions into rice. Arrange chicken over rice with meatiest parts toward edges of dish. Pour spaghetti sauce over chicken and rice. Cook, covered, 10 minutes, stirring rice halfway through cooking time. Rearrange chicken and rotate dish. Cook, covered, 9 to 10 minutes or until chicken and rice are done. Stir rice halfway through cooking time. Top chicken with remaining onions; cook, uncovered, 1 minute. Let stand 5 minutes.

TURKEY 'N STUFFING PIE

Ready to bake in just 12 easy minutes

1¼ cups water
¼ cup butter or margarine
3½ cups seasoned stuffing
    crumbs*
1 can (2.8 ounces) Durkee
    French Fried Onions
1 can (10¾ ounces) condensed
    cream of celery soup

¾ cup milk
1½ cups (7 ounces) cubed cooked
    turkey
1 package (10 ounces) frozen
    peas, thawed and drained

*3 cups leftover stuffing may be substituted for butter, water and stuffing crumbs. If stuffing is dry, stir in water, 1 tablespoon at a time, until moist but not wet.

(continued)

Turkey 'n Stuffing Pie

Preheat oven to 350°. In medium saucepan, heat water and butter; stir until butter melts. Remove from heat. Stir in seasoned stuffing crumbs and ½ *can* French Fried Onions. Spoon stuffing mixture into 9-inch round or fluted baking dish. Press stuffing evenly across bottom and up sides of dish to form a shell. In medium bowl, combine soup, milk, turkey and peas; pour into stuffing shell. Bake, covered, at 350° for 30 minutes or until heated through. Top with remaining onions; bake, uncovered, 5 minutes or until onions are golden brown.   *Makes 4 to 6 servings*

MICROWAVE DIRECTIONS: In 9-inch round or fluted microwave-safe dish, place water and butter. Cook, covered, on HIGH 3 minutes or until butter melts. Stir in stuffing crumbs and ½ *can* onions. Press stuffing mixture into dish as above. Reduce milk to ½ cup. In large microwave-safe bowl, combine soup, milk, turkey and peas; cook, covered, 8 minutes. Stir turkey mixture halfway through cooking time. Pour turkey mixture into stuffing shell. Cook, uncovered, 4 to 6 minutes or until heated through. Rotate dish halfway through cooking time. Top with remaining onions; cook, uncovered, 1 minute. Let stand 5 minutes.

ITALIAN ANTIPASTO BAKE

Ready to bake in just 10 easy minutes —————————

2 cups rotini or elbow
    macaroni, cooked in
    unsalted water and drained
1 bag (16 ounces) frozen
    vegetable combination
    (broccoli, water chestnuts,
    red pepper), thawed and
    drained
2 chicken breast halves,
    skinned, boned and cut
    into strips
⅔ cup bottled Italian salad
    dressing

½ cup drained garbanzo beans
    (optional)
¼ cup sliced pitted ripe olives
    (optional)
¼ cup (1 ounce) grated
    Parmesan cheese
½ teaspoon Italian seasoning
1 cup (4 ounces) shredded
    mozzarella cheese
1 can (2.8 ounces) Durkee
    French Fried Onions

Preheat oven to 350°. In 9×13-inch baking dish, combine hot pasta, vegetables, chicken, salad dressing, garbanzo beans, olives, Parmesan cheese and Italian seasoning. Stir in ½ *cup* mozzarella cheese and ½ *can* French Fried Onions. Bake, covered, at 350° for 35 minutes or until chicken is done. Top with remaining mozzarella cheese and onions; bake, uncovered, 5 minutes or until onions are golden brown.
Makes 4 to 6 servings

MICROWAVE DIRECTIONS: In 8×12-inch microwave-safe dish, combine ingredients, except chicken strips, as above. Arrange uncooked chicken strips around edges of dish. Cook, covered, on HIGH 6 minutes. Stir center of casserole; rearrange chicken and rotate dish. Cook, covered, 5 to 6 minutes or until chicken is done. Stir casserole to combine chicken and pasta mixture. Top with remaining mozzarella cheese and onions; cook, uncovered, 1 minute or until cheese melts. Let stand 5 minutes.

HOME-STYLE CHICKEN 'N BISCUITS

Ready to bake in just 15 easy minutes —————————

5 slices bacon, fried crisp and
    crumbled
1½ cups (7 ounces) cubed cooked
    chicken
1 package (10 ounces) frozen
    mixed vegetables, thawed
    and drained
1½ cups (6 ounces) shredded
    Cheddar cheese

2 medium tomatoes, chopped
    (about 1 cup)
1 can (10¾ ounces) condensed
    cream of chicken soup
¾ cup milk
1½ cups biscuit baking mix
⅔ cup milk
1 can (2.8 ounces) Durkee
    French Fried Onions

(continued)

Home-Style Chicken 'n Biscuits

Preheat oven to 400°. In large bowl, combine bacon, chicken, mixed vegetables, *1 cup* cheese, the tomatoes, soup and ¾ cup milk. Pour chicken mixture into greased 8×12-inch baking dish. Bake, covered, at 400° for 15 minutes. Meanwhile, in medium bowl, combine baking mix, ⅔ cup milk and ½ *can* French Fried Onions to form soft dough. Spoon biscuit dough in 6 mounds around edges of casserole. Bake, uncovered, 15 to 20 minutes or until biscuits are golden brown. Top biscuits with remaining cheese and onions; bake 1 to 3 minutes or until onions are golden brown.   *Makes 6 servings*

MICROWAVE DIRECTIONS: Prepare chicken mixture as above, except reduce ¾ cup milk to ½ cup; pour into 8×12-inch microwave-safe dish. Cook, covered, on HIGH 10 minutes or until heated through. Stir chicken mixture halfway through cooking time. Prepare biscuit dough as above. Stir casserole and spoon biscuit dough over hot chicken mixture as above. Cook, uncovered, 7 to 8 minutes or until biscuits are done. Rotate dish halfway through cooking time. Top biscuits with remaining cheese and onions; cook, uncovered, 1 minute or until cheese melts. Let stand 5 minutes.

NO-FUSS FISH & SEAFOOD

HERB-BAKED FISH & RICE

Ready to bake in just 15 easy minutes

1½ cups hot chicken bouillon
½ cup uncooked regular rice
¼ teaspoon Italian seasoning
¼ teaspoon garlic powder
1 package (10 ounces) frozen chopped broccoli, thawed and drained
1 can (2.8 ounces) Durkee French Fried Onions

1 tablespoon grated Parmesan cheese
1 pound unbreaded fish fillets, thawed if frozen
Paprika (optional)
½ cup (2 ounces) shredded Cheddar cheese

Preheat oven to 375°. In 8×12-inch baking dish, combine hot bouillon, uncooked rice and seasonings. Bake, covered, at 375° for 10 minutes. Top with broccoli, ½ *can* French Fried Onions and the Parmesan cheese. Place fish fillets diagonally down center of dish; sprinkle fish lightly with paprika. Bake, covered, at 375° for 20 to 25 minutes or until fish flakes easily with fork. Stir rice. Top fish with Cheddar cheese and remaining onions; bake, uncovered, 3 minutes or until onions are golden brown.   *Makes 3 to 4 servings*

MICROWAVE DIRECTIONS: In 8×12-inch microwave-safe dish, prepare rice mixture as above, except reduce bouillon to 1¼ cups. Cook, covered, on HIGH 5 minutes, stirring halfway through cooking time. Stir in broccoli, ½ *can* onions and the Parmesan cheese. Arrange fish fillets in single layer on top of rice mixture; sprinkle fish lightly with paprika. Cook, covered, on MEDIUM (50-60%) 18 to 20 minutes or until fish flakes easily with fork and rice is done. Rotate dish halfway through cooking time. Top fish with Cheddar cheese and remaining onions; cook, uncovered, on HIGH 1 minute or until cheese melts. Let stand 5 minutes.

HASTY SHORE DINNER

Ready to bake in just 7 easy minutes ━━━━━━━━

1 cup small shell pasta, cooked
    in unsalted water
    and drained
½ cup mayonnaise
½ cup milk
1 can (10¾ ounces) condensed
    cream of celery soup
1 package (8 ounces) frozen
    imitation crabmeat,*
    thawed, drained and cut
    into chunks

1 can (4 ounces) shrimp,
    drained
1 cup (4 ounces) shredded
    Swiss cheese
1 can (2.8 ounces) Durkee
    French Fried Onions
½ teaspoon dried dill weed,
    crumbled
¼ teaspoon seasoned salt

Preheat oven to 350°. Return hot pasta to saucepan. Stir in mayonnaise, milk, soup, crabmeat, shrimp, ½ *cup* cheese, ½ *can* French Fried Onions and the seasonings; mix well. Pour into 1½-quart casserole. Bake, covered, at 350° for 35 minutes or until heated through. Top with remaining cheese and onions; bake, uncovered, 5 minutes or until onions are golden brown.

Makes 4 to 6 servings

*1 can (6 ounces) crabmeat, drained, may be substituted for imitation crabmeat.

MICROWAVE DIRECTIONS: Prepare pasta mixture as above; pour into 1½-quart microwave-safe casserole. Cook, covered, on HIGH 12 to 15 minutes or until heated through. Stir casserole halfway through cooking time. Top with remaining cheese and onions; cook, uncovered, 1 minute or until cheese melts. Let stand 5 minutes.

SALMON LINGUINI SUPPER

Ready to bake in just 20 easy minutes ━━━━━━━━

8 ounces linguini, cooked in
    unsalted water and drained
1 package (10 ounces) frozen
    peas
1 cup milk
1 can (10¾ ounces) condensed
    cream of celery soup
¼ cup (1 ounce) grated
    Parmesan cheese
⅛ teaspoon dried tarragon,
    crumbled (optional)

1 can (15½ ounces) salmon,
    drained and flaked
1 egg, slightly beaten
¼ teaspoon salt
¼ teaspoon pepper
1 can (2.8 ounces) Durkee
    French Fried Onions

(continued)

Salmon Linguini Supper

Preheat oven to 375°. Return hot pasta to saucepan; stir in peas, milk, soup, cheese and tarragon; spoon into 8×12-inch baking dish. In medium bowl, using fork, combine salmon, egg, salt, pepper and ½ *can* French Fried Onions. Shape salmon mixture into 4 oval patties. Place patties on pasta mixture. Bake, covered, at 375° for 40 minutes or until patties are done. Top patties with remaining onions; bake, uncovered, 3 minutes or until onions are golden brown.   *Makes 4 servings*

MICROWAVE DIRECTIONS: Prepare pasta mixture as above, except increase milk to 1¼ cups; spoon into 8×12-inch microwave-safe dish. Cook, covered, on HIGH 3 minutes; stir. Prepare salmon patties as above using 2 eggs. Place patties on pasta mixture. Cook, covered, 10 to 12 minutes or until patties are done. Rotate dish halfway through cooking time. Top patties with remaining onions; cook, uncovered, 1 minute. Let stand 5 minutes.

SO-EASY FISH DIVAN

Ready to bake in just 10 easy minutes

1 package (about 1⅛ ounces) cheese sauce mix
1⅓ cups milk
1 bag (16 ounces) frozen vegetable combination (brussels sprouts, carrots, cauliflower), thawed and drained

1 can (2.8 ounces) Durkee French Fried Onions
1 pound unbreaded fish fillets, thawed if frozen
½ cup (2 ounces) shredded Cheddar cheese

Preheat oven to 375°. In small saucepan, prepare cheese sauce mix according to package directions using 1⅓ cups milk. In 8 × 12-inch baking dish, combine vegetables and ½ *can* French Fried Onions; top with fish fillets. Pour cheese sauce over fish and vegetables. Bake, covered, at 375° for 25 minutes or until fish flakes easily with fork. Top fish with Cheddar cheese and remaining onions; bake, uncovered, 3 minutes or until onions are golden brown.

Makes 3 to 4 servings

TUNA-SWISS PIE

Ready to bake in just 20 easy minutes

2 cups cooked unsalted regular rice (⅔ cup uncooked)
1 tablespoon butter or margarine
¼ teaspoon garlic powder
3 eggs
1 can (2.8 ounces) Durkee French Fried Onions

1 cup (4 ounces) shredded Swiss cheese
1 can (9¼ ounces) water-packed tuna, drained and flaked
1 cup milk
¼ teaspoon salt
¼ teaspoon pepper

Preheat oven to 400°. To hot rice in saucepan, add butter, garlic powder and *1 slightly beaten egg;* mix thoroughly. Spoon rice mixture into *ungreased* 9-inch pie plate. Press rice mixture firmly across bottom and up side of pie plate to form a crust. Layer ½ *can* French Fried Onions, ½ *cup* cheese and the tuna evenly over rice crust. In small bowl, combine milk, remaining eggs and the seasonings; pour over tuna filling. Bake, uncovered, at 400° for 30 to 35 minutes or until center is set. Top with remaining cheese and onions; bake, uncovered, 1 to 3 minutes or until onions are golden brown.

Makes 4 to 6 servings

TAG-ALONG TUNA BAKE

Refrigerate overnight; bake next day ━━━━━━━

3 to 4 tablespoons butter or
    margarine, softened
12 slices bread
1 can (12½ ounces) water-
    packed tuna, drained and
    flaked
1 cup chopped celery
1 can (2.8 ounces) Durkee
    French Fried Onions

2 cups milk
1 cup mayonnaise
4 eggs, slightly beaten
1 can (10¾ ounces) condensed
    cream of mushroom soup
3 slices (¾ ounce *each*)
    processed American
    cheese, cut diagonally into
    halves

Butter 1 side of each bread slice; arrange 6 slices, buttered-side down, in 9×13-inch baking dish. Layer tuna, celery and ½ *can* French Fried Onions evenly over bread. Top with remaining bread slices, buttered-side down. In medium bowl, combine milk, mayonnaise, eggs and soup; mix well. Pour evenly over layers in baking dish; cover and refrigerate overnight. Bake, covered, at 350° for 30 minutes. Uncover and bake 15 minutes or until center is set. Arrange cheese slices down center of casserole, overlapping slightly, points all in 1 direction. Top with remaining onions; bake, uncovered, 5 minutes or until onions are golden brown.

Makes 8 servings

FAST 'N FANCY STUFFED FLOUNDER

Ready to bake in just 10 easy minutes ━━━━━━━

1½ cups seasoned stuffing
    croutons
1 can (6 ounces) crabmeat,
    drained
1 can (2.8 ounces) Durkee
    French Fried Onions
¾ cup water
1 teaspoon instant chicken
    bouillon

1 pound unbreaded fish fillets,
    thawed if frozen
1 package (10 ounces) frozen
    asparagus spears, thawed
    and drained
Paprika

Preheat oven to 400°. In medium bowl, combine stuffing croutons, crabmeat, ½ *can* French Fried Onions, the water and bouillon; stir until well mixed. Place *half* the fish fillets in 8×12-inch baking dish; spoon stuffing over fish. Top stuffing with asparagus spears, then remaining fillets. Sprinkle fish lightly with paprika. Bake, covered, at 400° for 20 minutes or until fish flakes easily with fork. Top with remaining onions; bake, uncovered, 1 to 3 minutes or until onions are golden brown.

Makes 4 servings

MEDITERRANEAN FISH & PASTA

Ready to bake in just 15 easy minutes

2 cups gnocchi or large shell pasta, cooked in unsalted water and drained
1 can (14½ ounces) whole tomatoes, undrained and cut up
1 can (8 ounces) tomato sauce
1 medium zucchini, thinly sliced (about 1 cup)
½ cup (2 ounces) grated Parmesan cheese
1 can (2.8 ounces) Durkee French Fried Onions
⅓ cup sliced pitted ripe olives
½ teaspoon dried basil, crumbled
½ teaspoon dried oregano, crumbled
1 pound unbreaded fish fillets, thawed if frozen

Preheat oven to 375°. Return hot pasta to saucepan; stir in tomatoes, tomato sauce, zucchini, *¼ cup* cheese, *½ can* French Fried Onions, the olives and seasonings. Pour into 8×12-inch baking dish. Place fish fillets, in single layer, over pasta mixture. Bake, covered, at 375° for 25 minutes or until fish flakes easily with fork. Top with remaining cheese and onions; bake, uncovered, 3 minutes or until onions are golden brown. *Makes 3 to 4 servings*

MICROWAVE DIRECTIONS: Prepare pasta mixture as above; pour into 8×12-inch microwave-safe dish. Top with fish fillets as above. Cook, covered, on HIGH 10 to 12 minutes or until heated through and fish flakes easily with fork. Rotate dish halfway through cooking time. Top with remaining cheese and onions; cook, uncovered, 1 minute. Let stand 5 minutes.

TUNA TORTILLA ROLL-UPS

Ready to bake in just 20 easy minutes

1 can (10¾ ounces) condensed cream of celery soup
1 cup milk
1 can (9¼ ounces) tuna, drained and flaked
1 package (10 ounces) frozen broccoli spears, thawed, drained and cut into 1-inch pieces
1 cup (4 ounces) shredded Cheddar cheese
1 can (2.8 ounces) Durkee French Fried Onions
6 (7-inch) flour or corn tortillas
1 medium tomato, chopped

Preheat oven to 350°. In small bowl, combine soup and milk; set aside. In medium bowl, combine tuna, broccoli, *½ cup* cheese and *½ can* French Fried Onions; stir in *¾ cup* soup mixture. Divide tuna

(continued)

Tuna Tortilla Roll-Ups

mixture evenly between tortillas; roll up tortillas. Place, seam-side down, in lightly greased 9×13-inch baking dish. Stir tomato into remaining soup mixture; pour down center of roll-ups. Bake, covered, at 350° for 35 minutes or until heated through. Top center of roll-ups with remaining cheese and onions; bake, uncovered, 5 minutes or until onions are golden brown.   *Makes 6 servings*

MICROWAVE DIRECTIONS: Use corn tortillas only. Prepare soup mixture and roll-ups as above; place roll-ups, seam-side down, in 8×12-inch microwave-safe dish. Stir tomato into remaining soup mixture; pour down center of roll-ups. Cook, covered, on HIGH 15 to 18 minutes or until heated through. Rotate dish halfway through cooking time. Top center of roll-ups with remaining cheese and onions; cook, uncovered, 1 minute or until cheese melts. Let stand 5 minutes.

LOUISIANA SEAFOOD BAKE

Ready to bake in just 15 easy minutes

⅔ cup uncooked regular rice
1 cup sliced celery
1 cup water
1 can (14½ ounces) whole
    tomatoes, undrained and
    cut up
1 can (8 ounces) tomato
    sauce
1 can (2.8 ounces) Durkee
    French Fried Onions
1 teaspoon Durkee RedHot
    Cayenne Pepper Sauce
½ teaspoon garlic powder

¼ teaspoon dried oregano,
    crumbled
¼ teaspoon dried thyme,
    crumbled
½ pound white fish, thawed if
    frozen and cut into 1-inch
    chunks
1 can (4 ounces) shrimp,
    drained
⅓ cup sliced pitted ripe olives
¼ cup (1 ounce) grated
    Parmesan cheese

Preheat oven to 375°. In 1½-quart casserole, combine uncooked rice, celery, water, tomatoes, tomato sauce, ½ *can* French Fried Onions and the seasonings. Bake, covered, at 375° for 20 minutes. Stir in fish, shrimp and olives. Bake, covered, 20 minutes or until heated through. Top with cheese and remaining onions; bake, uncovered, 3 minutes or until onions are golden brown.   *Makes 4 servings*

MICROWAVE DIRECTIONS: In 2-quart microwave-safe casserole, prepare rice mixture as above. Cook, covered, on HIGH 15 minutes, stirring rice halfway through cooking time. Add fish, shrimp and olives. Cook, covered, 12 to 14 minutes or until rice is cooked. Stir casserole halfway through cooking time. Top with cheese and remaining onions; cook, uncovered, 1 minute. Let stand 5 minutes.

SUPERB FILLET OF SOLE & VEGETABLES

Ready to bake in just 10 easy minutes

1 can (10¾ ounces) condensed
    cream of celery soup
½ cup milk
1 cup (4 ounces) shredded
    Swiss cheese
½ teaspoon dried basil,
    crumbled
¼ teaspoon seasoned salt
¼ teaspoon pepper

1 package (10 ounces) frozen
    baby carrots, thawed and
    drained
1 package (10 ounces) frozen
    asparagus cuts, thawed and
    drained
1 can (2.8 ounces) Durkee
    French Fried Onions
1 pound unbreaded sole fillets,
    thawed if frozen

Preheat oven to 375°. In small bowl, combine soup, milk, ½ *cup* cheese and the seasonings; set aside. In 8 × 12-inch baking dish,

(continued)

Superb Fillet of Sole & Vegetables

combine carrots, asparagus and *½ can* French Fried Onions. Roll up fish fillets. (If fillets are wide, fold in half lengthwise before rolling.) Place fish rolls upright along center of vegetable mixture. Pour soup mixture over fish and vegetables. Bake, covered, at 375° for 30 minutes or until fish flakes easily with fork. Stir vegetables; top fish with remaining cheese and onions. Bake, uncovered, 3 minutes or until onions are golden brown.   *Makes 3 to 4 servings*

MICROWAVE DIRECTIONS: Prepare soup mixture as above; set aside. In 8×12-inch microwave-safe dish, combine vegetables as above. Roll up fish fillets as above; place upright around edges of dish. Pour soup mixture over fish and vegetables. Cook, covered, on HIGH 14 to 16 minutes or until fish flakes easily with fork. Stir vegetables and rotate dish halfway through cooking time. Top fish with remaining cheese and onions; cook, uncovered, 1 minute or until cheese melts. Let stand 5 minutes.

FOOLPROOF CLAM FETTUCINE

Ready to bake in just 15 easy minutes

1 package (6 ounces) fettucine-
   style noodles with creamy
   cheese sauce mix
¾ cup milk
1 can (6½ ounces) chopped
   clams, undrained
¼ cup (1 ounce) grated
   Parmesan cheese

1 teaspoon parsley flakes
1 can (4 ounces) mushroom
   stems and pieces, drained
2 tablespoons diced pimiento
1 can (2.8 ounces) Durkee
   French Fried Onions

Preheat oven to 375°. In large saucepan, cook noodles according to package directions; drain. Return hot noodles to saucepan; stir in sauce mix, milk, undrained clams, Parmesan cheese, parsley flakes, mushrooms, pimiento and *½ can* French Fried Onions. Heat and stir 3 minutes or until bubbly. Pour into 6 × 10-inch baking dish. Bake, covered, at 375° for 30 minutes or until thickened. Place remaining onions around edges of casserole; bake, uncovered, 3 minutes or until onions are golden brown. *Makes 4 servings*

MICROWAVE DIRECTIONS: Prepare noodle mixture as above; pour into 6 × 10-inch microwave-safe dish. Cook, covered, on HIGH 4 to 6 minutes or until heated through. Stir noodle mixture halfway through cooking time. Top with remaining onions as above; cook, uncovered, 1 minute. Let stand 5 minutes.

TUNA LASAGNA BUNDLES

Ready to bake in just 20 easy minutes

6 lasagna noodles, cooked in
   unsalted water and drained
1 can (10¾ ounces) condensed
   cream of chicken soup
½ cup milk
1 can (6½ ounces) tuna, drained
   and flaked
1 package (10 ounces) frozen
   chopped spinach or
   broccoli, thawed and well
   drained

1 egg, slightly beaten
¼ cup dry seasoned bread
   crumbs
¼ teaspoon garlic salt
1 cup (4 ounces) shredded
   Cheddar cheese
1 can (2.8 ounces) Durkee
   French Fried Onions

Preheat oven to 350°. Place hot noodles under cold running water until cool enough to handle; drain and set aside. In small bowl, blend soup and milk; set aside. In medium bowl, combine tuna, spinach, egg, bread crumbs, garlic salt, *½ cup* cheese and *½ can*

(continued)

French Fried Onions; stir in ½ cup soup mixture. Cut cooled noodles crosswise into halves. Spoon equal amounts of tuna mixture onto center of each noodle; roll up noodles. Place tuna rolls, seam-side down, in greased 8 × 12-inch baking dish. Top with remaining soup mixture. Bake, covered, at 350° for 35 minutes or until heated through. Top with remaining cheese and onions; bake, uncovered, 5 minutes or until onions are golden brown.   *Makes 6 servings*

MICROWAVE DIRECTIONS: Prepare soup mixture and tuna rolls as above. Place rolls, seam-side down, in 8 × 12-inch microwave-safe dish; top with remaining soup mixture. Cook, covered, on HIGH 10 to 12 minutes or until heated through. Rotate dish halfway through cooking time. Top tuna rolls with remaining cheese and onions; cook, uncovered, 1 minute or until cheese melts. Let stand 5 minutes.

CRUNCHY-TOPPED FISH & VEGETABLES

Ready to bake in just 10 easy minutes ━━━━━━━━

1 can (16 ounces) whole potatoes, drained
1 bag (16 ounces) frozen vegetable combination (broccoli, carrots, red pepper, water chestnuts), thawed and drained
⅓ cup water
2 tablespoons bottled Italian salad dressing

1 cup (4 ounces) shredded Cheddar cheese
⅓ cup dry bread crumbs
1 can (2.8 ounces) Durkee French Fried Onions
2 tablespoons water
½ teaspoon dried dill weed, crumbled
1 pound unbreaded fish fillets, thawed if frozen

Preheat oven to 375°. Place potatoes and vegetables in 8 × 12-inch baking dish; drizzle with ⅓ cup water and the Italian salad dressing. In small bowl, using fork, combine ½ cup cheese, the bread crumbs, French Fried Onions, 2 tablespoons water and the dill weed; mix thoroughly to crush onions. Sprinkle *half* the onion mixture evenly over vegetables. Arrange fish fillets over vegetables. Top fish with remaining cheese, then sprinkle with remaining onion mixture. Bake, uncovered, at 375° for 20 to 25 minutes or until fish flakes easily with fork.   *Makes 4 servings*

MICROWAVE DIRECTIONS: Omit ⅓ cup water. Place potatoes and vegetables in 8 × 12-inch microwave-safe dish; drizzle with Italian salad dressing. Prepare onion mixture and layer with fish and remaining cheese in dish as above. Cook, uncovered, on HIGH 13 to 15 minutes or until fish flakes easily with fork. Rotate dish halfway through cooking time. Let stand 5 minutes.

BUSY-DAY BEEF

COUNTDOWN CASSEROLE

Ready to bake in just 10 easy minutes

1 jar (8 ounces) pasteurized
   processed cheese
   spread
¾ cup milk
2 cups (12 ounces) cubed
   cooked roast beef
1 bag (16 ounces) frozen
   vegetable combination
   (broccoli, corn, red pepper),
   thawed and drained

4 cups frozen hash brown
   potatoes, thawed
1 can (2.8 ounces) Durkee
   French Fried Onions
½ teaspoon seasoned salt
¼ teaspoon black pepper
½ cup (2 ounces) shredded
   Cheddar cheese

Preheat oven to 375°. Spoon cheese spread into 8×12-inch baking dish; place in oven just until cheese melts, about 5 minutes. Using fork, stir milk into melted cheese until well blended. Stir in beef, vegetables, potatoes, *½ can* French Fried Onions and the seasonings. Bake, covered, at 375° for 30 minutes or until heated through. Top with Cheddar cheese and sprinkle onions down center. Bake, uncovered, 3 minutes or until onions are golden brown.

Makes 4 to 6 servings

MICROWAVE DIRECTIONS: In an 8×12-inch microwave-safe dish, combine cheese spread and milk. Cook, covered, on HIGH 3 minutes; stir. Add ingredients as above. Cook, covered, 14 minutes or until heated through. Stir beef mixture halfway through cooking time. Top with Cheddar cheese and remaining onions as above. Cook, uncovered, 1 minute or until cheese melts. Let stand 5 minutes.

HASH-AND-EGG BRUNCH

Ready to bake in just 8 easy minutes

1 can (12 ounces) corned beef,
   cut into chunks
3 cups frozen hash brown
   potatoes, thawed
1 can (10¾ ounces)
   condensed cream
   of celery soup

1 can (2.8 ounces) Durkee
   French Fried Onions
¼ teaspoon pepper
6 eggs
½ cup (2 ounces) shredded
   Cheddar cheese

Preheat oven to 400°. In large bowl, combine corned beef, potatoes, soup, ½ *can* French Fried Onions and the pepper. Spoon evenly into 8×12-inch baking dish. Bake, covered, at 400° for 20 minutes or until heated through. Using back of spoon, make 6 wells in hash mixture. Break 1 egg into each well. Bake, uncovered, 15 to 20 minutes or until eggs are cooked to desired doneness. Sprinkle cheese down center of dish and top with remaining onions. Bake, uncovered, 1 to 3 minutes or until onions are golden brown.

Makes 6 servings

MICROWAVE DIRECTIONS: Prepare corned beef mixture as above; spoon into 8×12-inch microwave-safe dish. Do not add eggs. Cook, uncovered, on HIGH 10 minutes. Rotate dish halfway through cooking time. Place eggs in hash as above. Using a toothpick, pierce each egg yolk and white twice. Cook, covered, 5 to 6 minutes or until eggs are cooked to desired doneness. Rotate dish halfway through cooking time. Top with cheese and remaining onions; cook, uncovered, 1 minute or until cheese melts. Let stand 5 minutes.

CORN BREAD TACO BAKE

Ready to bake in just 12 easy minutes

1½ pounds ground beef
1 package (about 1⅛ ounces)
   taco seasoning mix
½ cup water
1 can (12 ounces) whole kernel
   corn, drained
½ cup chopped green pepper
1 can (8 ounces) tomato sauce

1 package (8½ ounces) corn
   muffin mix, plus
   ingredients to prepare mix
1 can (2.8 ounces) Durkee
   French Fried Onions
½ cup (2 ounces) shredded
   Cheddar cheese

Preheat oven to 400°. In large skillet, brown ground beef; drain. Stir in taco seasoning, water, corn, green pepper and tomato sauce; pour mixture into 2-quart casserole. In small bowl, prepare corn muffin mix according to package directions; stir in ½ *can* French Fried

(continued)

Corn Bread Taco Bake

Onions. Spoon corn muffin batter around edge of beef mixture.
Bake, uncovered, at 400° for 20 minutes or until corn bread is done.
Top corn bread with cheese and remaining onions; bake, uncovered,
1 to 3 minutes or until onions are golden brown.

Makes 6 servings

MICROWAVE DIRECTIONS: Crumble ground beef into 8 × 12-inch
microwave-safe dish. Cook, covered, on HIGH 4 to 6 minutes or
until beef is cooked. Stir beef halfway through cooking time. Drain
well. Prepare beef mixture and top with corn muffin batter as above.
Cook, uncovered, on MEDIUM (50-60%) 7 to 9 minutes or until
corn bread is nearly done. Rotate dish halfway through cooking
time. Top corn bread with cheese and remaining onions; cook,
uncovered, on HIGH 1 minute or until cheese melts. Cover
casserole and let stand 10 minutes. (Corn bread will finish baking
during standing time.)

SPEEDY CHILI-MAC

Ready to bake in just 5 easy minutes

2 cups elbow macaroni, cooked in unsalted water and drained
1 can (10¾ ounces) condensed cream of mushroom soup

1 can (15 ounces) chili without beans
1 cup (4 ounces) shredded Cheddar cheese
1 can (2.8 ounces) Durkee French Fried Onions

Preheat oven to 350°. Return hot macaroni to saucepan; stir in soup, chili, ½ cup cheese and ½ can French Fried Onions. Spoon macaroni mixture into greased 2-quart casserole. Bake, covered, at 350° for 25 minutes or until heated through. Top with remaining cheese and onions; bake, uncovered, 5 minutes or until onions are golden brown.   *Makes 4 to 6 servings*

MICROWAVE DIRECTIONS: Prepare macaroni mixture as above; spoon into 2-quart microwave-safe casserole. Cook, covered, on HIGH 8 to 10 minutes or until heated through, stirring mixture halfway through cooking time. Stir casserole; top with remaining cheese and onions. Cook, uncovered, 1 minute or until cheese melts. Let stand 5 minutes.

FAST 'N FUN PASTA PIZZA

Ready to bake in just 15 easy minutes

3 cups fusilli or elbow macaroni, cooked in unsalted water and drained
1 pound ground beef
1 jar (15½ ounces) spaghetti sauce
2 eggs, slightly beaten
1 can (2.8 ounces) Durkee French Fried Onions

⅓ cup (about 1½ ounces) grated Parmesan cheese
Assorted toppings: chopped green pepper, sliced mushrooms, sliced pitted ripe olives
1 cup (4 ounces) shredded mozzarella cheese

Preheat oven to 375°. In medium skillet, brown ground beef; drain. Stir in spaghetti sauce; reduce heat and simmer, uncovered, 5 minutes. In medium bowl, combine hot pasta, eggs, ½ can French Fried Onions and the Parmesan cheese. Spread pasta mixture over greased 12-inch pizza pan. Top with ground beef mixture and desired toppings. Bake, covered, at 375° for 25 minutes or until heated through. Top with mozzarella cheese and remaining onions; bake, uncovered, 3 minutes or until onions are golden brown. Cut into wedges to serve.   *Makes 4 to 6 servings*

OVEN-EASY BEEF & POTATO DINNER

Ready to bake in just 15 easy minutes

4 cups frozen hash brown
    potatoes, thawed
3 tablespoons vegetable oil
⅛ teaspoon pepper
1 pound ground beef
1 cup water
1 package (about ¾ ounce)
    brown gravy mix
½ teaspoon garlic salt

1 package (10 ounces) frozen
    mixed vegetables, thawed
    and drained
1 cup (4 ounces) shredded
    Cheddar cheese
1 can (2.8 ounces) Durkee
    French Fried Onions

Preheat oven to 400°. In 8×12-inch baking dish, combine potatoes, oil and pepper. Firmly press potato mixture evenly across bottom and up sides of dish to form a shell. Bake, uncovered, at 400° for 15 minutes. Meanwhile, in large skillet, brown ground beef; drain. Stir in water, gravy mix and garlic salt; bring to a boil. Add mixed vegetables; reduce heat to medium and cook, uncovered, 5 minutes. Remove from heat and stir in ½ *cup* cheese and ½ *can* French Fried Onions; spoon into hot potato shell. Reduce oven temperature to 350°. Bake, uncovered, at 350° for 15 minutes or until heated through. Top with remaining cheese and onions; bake, uncovered, 5 minutes or until onions are golden brown.   *Makes 4 to 6 servings*

Oven-Easy Beef & Potato Dinner

AWARD-WINNING MEXICALI CASSEROLE

Ready to bake in just 15 easy minutes

2 cups elbow macaroni, cooked in unsalted water and drained
1 pound ground beef
1 package (about 1⅛ ounces) taco seasoning mix
1 can (15 ounces) chili beans or kidney beans, undrained
1 can (15 ounces) tomato sauce
¼ cup milk
2½ cups (10 ounces) shredded sharp Cheddar cheese
1 can (2.8 ounces) Durkee French Fried Onions
1 cup shredded lettuce
1 medium tomato, diced

Preheat oven to 375°. In medium skillet, brown ground beef; drain. Stir in taco seasoning, beans and tomato sauce. Reduce heat and simmer, uncovered, 5 minutes. Return hot macaroni to saucepan; stir in milk and *2 cups* cheese. In greased 3-quart casserole, layer *half* the macaroni, *half* the meat mixture and *½ can* French Fried Onions. Top with remaining macaroni, then with remaining meat mixture. Bake, uncovered, at 375° for 20 to 25 minutes or until heated through. Top with remaining cheese and onions; bake, uncovered, 3 minutes or until onions are golden brown. Serve garnished with lettuce and tomato. *Makes 6 to 8 servings*

OLD-FASHIONED BEEF POT PIE

Ready to bake in just 15 easy minutes

1 pound ground beef
1 can (11 ounces) condensed beef with vegetables and barley soup
½ cup water
1 package (10 ounces) frozen peas and carrots, thawed and drained
½ teaspoon seasoned salt
⅛ teaspoon garlic powder
⅛ teaspoon pepper
1 cup (4 ounces) shredded Cheddar cheese
1 can (2.8 ounces) Durkee French Fried Onions
1 package (7.5 ounces) refrigerated biscuits

Preheat oven to 350°. In large skillet, brown ground beef leaving in large chunks; drain. Stir in soup, water, vegetables and seasonings; bring to a boil. Reduce heat and simmer, uncovered, 5 minutes. Remove from heat; stir in *½ cup* cheese and *½ can* French Fried Onions. Pour into 8×12-inch baking dish. Cut each biscuit in half; place, cut-side down, around edge of casserole. Bake, uncovered, at 350° for 15 to 20 minutes or until biscuits are done. Top with remaining cheese and onions; bake, uncovered, 5 minutes or until onions are golden brown. *Makes 4 to 6 servings*

COTTAGE BEEF & EGGPLANT

Ready to bake in just 20 easy minutes ———————

1 pound ground beef
1 medium green pepper, cut into ½-inch chunks
1 can (14½ ounces) whole tomatoes, undrained and cut up
1 can (6 ounces) tomato paste
½ teaspoon dried oregano, crumbled
½ teaspoon salt

1½ cups (12 ounces) cream-style cottage cheese
1 can (2.8 ounces) Durkee French Fried Onions
1 egg, slightly beaten
1 medium eggplant, cut into ½-inch slices
¼ cup (1 ounce) grated Parmesan cheese

Preheat oven to 375°. In large skillet, brown ground beef; drain. Add green pepper and cook until tender-crisp. Stir in tomatoes, tomato paste and seasonings; set aside. In medium bowl, combine cottage cheese, *½ can* French Fried Onions and the egg; mix until well blended. Arrange eggplant slices in bottom of 9×13-inch baking dish. Spoon meat sauce over eggplant, then top with cottage cheese mixture. Bake, covered, at 375° for 35 minutes or until heated through. Top with Parmesan cheese and remaining onions; bake, uncovered, 3 minutes or until onions are golden brown.

Makes 6 servings

MICROWAVE DIRECTIONS: Crumble ground beef into medium microwave-safe bowl; add green pepper. Cook, covered, on HIGH 4 to 6 minutes or until beef is cooked. Stir beef halfway through cooking time. Drain well. Stir in tomatoes, tomato paste and seasonings. Prepare cottage cheese mixture as above. In 8×12-inch microwave-safe dish, layer eggplant, meat sauce and cottage cheese mixture as above. (Eggplant slices may overlap slightly.) Cook, covered, 18 to 20 minutes or until heated through. Rotate dish halfway through cooking time. Top with Parmesan cheese and remaining onions; cook, uncovered, 1 minute. Let stand 5 minutes.

CHEESE-STUFFED BEEF ROLLS

Ready to bake in just 15 easy minutes

1 jar (15½ ounces) spaghetti
    sauce
1 egg, slightly beaten
¼ teaspoon dried oregano,
    crumbled
¼ teaspoon garlic powder
1 container (15 ounces) ricotta
    cheese
¼ cup (1 ounce) grated
    Parmesan cheese

1 cup (4 ounces) shredded
    mozzarella cheese
1 can (2.8 ounces) Durkee
    French Fried Onions
6 thin slices deli roast beef
    (about ½ pound)
2 medium zucchini, sliced
    (about 3 cups)

Preheat oven to 375°. Spread *½ cup* spaghetti sauce in bottom of 8×12-inch baking dish. In large bowl, thoroughly combine egg, seasonings, ricotta cheese, Parmesan cheese, *½ cup* mozzarella cheese and *½ can* French Fried Onions. Spoon equal amounts of cheese mixture on 1 end of each beef slice. Roll up beef slices jelly-roll style and arrange, seam-side down, in baking dish. Place zucchini along both sides of dish. Pour remaining spaghetti sauce over beef rolls and zucchini. Bake, covered, at 375° for 40 minutes or until heated through. Top beef rolls with remaining mozzarella cheese and onions. Bake, uncovered, 3 minutes or until onions are golden brown.

Makes 6 servings

MICROWAVE DIRECTIONS: In large microwave-safe bowl, prepare cheese mixture as above. Cook, covered, on HIGH 2 to 4 minutes or until warmed through. Stir cheese mixture halfway through cooking time. Spread *½ cup* spaghetti sauce in bottom of 8×12-inch microwave-safe dish. Prepare beef rolls and place in dish as above. Arrange zucchini along both sides of dish. Pour remaining spaghetti sauce over beef rolls and zucchini. Cook, loosely covered, 14 to 16 minutes or until heated through. Rotate dish halfway through cooking time. Top beef rolls with remaining mozzarella cheese and onions; cook, uncovered, 1 minute or until cheese melts. Let stand 5 minutes.

TWISTY BEEF BAKE

Ready to bake in just 10 easy minutes ─────────────

2 cups rotini or elbow
    macaroni, cooked in
    unsalted water and
    drained
1 pound ground beef
1 can (2.8 ounces) Durkee
    French Fried Onions
1 cup (4 ounces) shredded
    Cheddar cheese

1 can (10¾ ounces) condensed
    cream of mushroom soup
1 can (14½ ounces) whole
    tomatoes, undrained and
    cut up
¼ cup chopped green pepper
¼ teaspoon seasoned salt

Preheat oven to 375°. In large skillet, brown ground beef; drain. Stir in hot macaroni, *½ can* French Fried Onions, *½ cup* cheese, the soup, tomatoes, green pepper and seasoned salt. Mix well. Pour into 2-quart casserole. Bake, covered, at 375° for 30 minutes or until heated through. Top with remaining cheese and onions; bake, uncovered, 3 minutes or until onions are golden brown.

Makes 4 to 6 servings

MICROWAVE DIRECTIONS: Crumble ground beef into 2-quart microwave-safe casserole. Cook, covered, on HIGH 4 to 6 minutes or until beef is cooked. Stir beef halfway through cooking time. Drain well. Add remaining ingredients as above. Cook, covered, 10 to 14 minutes or until heated through. Stir beef mixture halfway through cooking time. Top with remaining cheese and onions; cook, uncovered, 1 minute or until cheese melts. Let stand 5 minutes.

MINI MEAT LOAVES & VEGETABLES

Ready to bake in just 10 easy minutes ─────────────

1½ pounds lean ground beef
1 egg
1 can (8 ounces) tomato sauce
1 can (2.8 ounces) Durkee
    French Fried Onions
½ teaspoon salt
½ teaspoon Italian seasoning

6 small red potatoes, thinly
    sliced (about 1½ cups)
1 bag (16 ounces) frozen
    vegetable combination
    (broccoli, corn, red pepper),
    thawed and drained
Salt
Black pepper

Preheat oven to 375°. In medium bowl, combine ground beef, egg, *½ can* tomato sauce, *½ can* French Fried Onions, ½ teaspoon salt and Italian seasoning. Shape into 3 mini loaves and place in 9×13-inch baking dish. Arrange potatoes around loaves. Bake, covered, at 375° for 35 minutes. Spoon vegetables around meat loaves; stir to

(continued)

Mini Meat Loaves & Vegetables

combine with potatoes. Lightly season vegetables with salt and pepper, if desired. Top meat loaves with remaining tomato sauce. Bake, uncovered, 15 minutes or until meat loaves are done. Top loaves with remaining onions; bake, uncovered, 3 minutes or until onions are golden brown. *Makes 6 servings*

MICROWAVE DIRECTIONS: Prepare meat loaves as above. Arrange potatoes on bottom of 8×12-inch microwave-safe dish; place meat loaves on potatoes. Cook, covered, on HIGH 13 minutes. Rotate dish halfway through cooking time. Add vegetables and season as above. Top meat loaves with remaining tomato sauce. Cook, covered, 7 minutes or until meat loaves are done. Rotate dish halfway through cooking time. Top loaves with remaining onions; cook, uncovered, 1 minute. Let stand 5 minutes.

TEXAS CHILI & BISCUITS

Ready to bake in just 18 easy minutes

1 pound ground beef
1 package (about 1¾ ounces) chili seasoning mix
1 can (16 ounces) whole kernel corn, drained
1 can (14½ ounces) whole tomatoes, undrained and cut up

½ cup water
¾ cup biscuit baking mix
⅔ cup cornmeal
⅔ cup milk
1 can (2.8 ounces) Durkee French Fried Onions
½ cup (2 ounces) shredded Monterey Jack cheese

Preheat oven to 400°. In medium skillet, brown ground beef; drain. Stir in chili seasoning, corn, tomatoes and water; bring to a boil. Reduce heat and simmer, uncovered, 10 minutes. Meanwhile, in medium bowl, combine baking mix, cornmeal, milk and ½ can French Fried Onions; beat vigorously 30 seconds. Pour chili into 2-quart casserole. Spoon biscuit dough in mounds around edge of casserole. Bake, uncovered, at 400° for 15 minutes or until biscuits are light brown. Top biscuits with cheese and remaining onions; bake, uncovered, 1 to 3 minutes or until onions are golden brown.

Makes 4 to 6 servings

GIANT STUFFED PEPPER

Ready to bake in just 15 easy minutes

1 cup cooked unsalted regular rice (⅓ cup uncooked)
2 large or 3 medium green peppers
1 pound ground beef
1 can (10¾ ounces) condensed tomato soup

2 teaspoons Worcestershire sauce
⅛ teaspoon black pepper
¾ cup (3 ounces) shredded Swiss cheese
1 can (2.8 ounces) Durkee French Fried Onions

Preheat oven to 375°. In medium saucepan, bring 1 quart water to a boil. Remove tops and seeds from green peppers; cut lengthwise into quarters. Cook pepper quarters in boiling water for 4 to 5 minutes or until tender-crisp; drain. Arrange pepper quarters around sides of 1½-quart casserole, forming a shell. In large skillet, brown ground beef; drain. Stir in soup, hot rice, Worcestershire sauce, black pepper, ½ cup cheese and ½ can French Fried Onions. Spoon meat mixture into green-pepper-lined casserole. Bake, covered, at 375° for 35 minutes or until heated through. Top with remaining cheese and onions; bake, uncovered, 3 minutes or until onions are golden brown.

Makes 4 servings

Layered Italian Beef

Ready to bake in just 15 easy minutes

3 cups rotini or elbow
    macaroni, cooked in
    unsalted water and drained
1 pound ground beef
1 jar (32 ounces) spaghetti
    sauce
1 cup (8 ounces) ricotta cheese

½ cup sour cream
1 teaspoon garlic salt
¼ teaspoon dried oregano,
    crumbled
1 can (2.8 ounces) Durkee
    French Fried Onions

Preheat oven to 350°. In medium skillet, brown ground beef; drain. Stir in spaghetti sauce; reduce heat and simmer, uncovered, 5 minutes. In small bowl, thoroughly blend ricotta cheese, sour cream and seasonings. Return hot macaroni to saucepan. Stir in ½ can French Fried Onions; spread evenly in bottom of 8×12-inch baking dish. Pour *half* the meat sauce over macaroni; cover with cheese mixture. Pour remaining meat sauce over top. Bake, covered, at 350° for 25 minutes or until heated through. Top with remaining onions; bake, uncovered, 5 minutes or until onions are golden brown.

Makes 6 to 8 servings

Fiesta Casserole

Ready to bake in just 12 easy minutes

1 pound ground beef
1 medium green pepper,
    chopped
2 cans (8 ounces *each*) tomato
    sauce
¼ cup water
1 can (12 ounces) whole kernel
    corn with sweet peppers,
    drained
1 tablespoon chili powder
½ teaspoon garlic salt

⅛ teaspoon crushed red pepper
    flakes (optional)
1 can (2.8 ounces) Durkee
    French Fried Onions
1 package (10 ounces)
    refrigerated biscuits
½ cup (2 ounces) shredded
    Cheddar cheese

Preheat oven to 350°. In large skillet, brown ground beef; drain. Add green pepper and cook until tender-crisp. Stir in tomato sauce, water, corn, seasonings and ½ can French Fried Onions. Reduce heat and simmer, uncovered, until heated through. Spoon beef mixture into greased 8×12-inch baking dish. Cut biscuits in half; arrange around baking dish so cut edges face sides of dish and ends overlap. Bake, uncovered, at 350° for 15 to 20 minutes or until biscuits are done. Top with cheese and remaining onions; bake, uncovered, 5 minutes or until onions are golden brown. *Makes 6 servings*

FIX-IT-FAST CORNED BEEF & CABBAGE

Ready to bake in just 15 easy minutes ━━━━━━━━━━

1 small head cabbage (about
    1½ pounds), cored and cut
    into 6 wedges
1 can (12 ounces) corned beef,
    sliced or ½ pound sliced
    deli corned beef
1 can (14 ounces) sliced carrots,
    drained

1 can (16 ounces) sliced
    potatoes, drained
1 can (2.8 ounces) Durkee
    French Fried Onions
1 can (10¾ ounces) condensed
    cream of celery soup
¾ cup water

Preheat oven to 375°. Arrange cabbage wedges and corned beef slices alternately down center of 9×13-inch baking dish. Place carrots, potatoes and ½ *can* French Fried Onions along sides of dish. In small bowl, combine soup and water; pour over meat and vegetables. Bake, covered, at 375° for 40 minutes or until cabbage is tender. Top with remaining onions; bake, uncovered, 3 minutes or until onions are golden brown. *Makes 4 to 6 servings*

MICROWAVE DIRECTIONS: Arrange cabbage wedges down center of 8×12-inch microwave-safe dish; add 2 tablespoons water. Cook, covered, on HIGH 10 to 12 minutes or until fork tender. Rotate the dish halfway through cooking time. Drain. Arrange cabbage, corned beef, carrots, potatoes and ½ *can* onions in dish as above. Reduce water to ¼ cup. In small bowl, combine soup and water; pour over meat and vegetables. Cook, covered, 8 to 10 minutes or until vegetables are heated through. Rotate the dish halfway through cooking time. Top with remaining onions; cook, uncovered, 1 minute. Let stand 5 minutes.

MEXICAN STUFFED SHELLS

Ready to bake in just 15 easy minutes ━━━━━━━━━━

12 pasta stuffing shells, cooked
    in unsalted water and
    drained
1 pound ground beef
1 jar (12 ounces) mild or
    medium picante sauce
½ cup water

1 can (8 ounces) tomato sauce
1 can (4 ounces) chopped green
    chilies, drained
1 cup (4 ounces) shredded
    Monterey Jack cheese
1 can (2.8 ounces) Durkee
    French Fried Onions

Preheat oven to 350°. In large skillet, brown ground beef; drain. In small bowl, combine picante sauce, water and tomato sauce. Stir ½ *cup* sauce mixture into beef along with chilies, ½ cup cheese and ½ *can* French Fried Onions; mix well. Spread *half* the remaining sauce

(continued)

Mexican Stuffed Shells

mixture in bottom of 10-inch round baking dish. Stuff cooked shells with beef mixture. Arrange shells in baking dish; top with remaining sauce. Bake, covered, at 350° for 30 minutes or until heated through. Top with remaining cheese and onions; bake, uncovered, 5 minutes or until onions are golden brown.

Makes 6 servings

MICROWAVE DIRECTIONS: Crumble ground beef into medium microwave-safe bowl. Cook, covered, on HIGH 4 to 6 minutes or until beef is cooked. Stir beef halfway through cooking time. Drain well. Prepare sauce mixture as above; spread ½ *cup* in 8×12-inch microwave-safe dish. Prepare beef mixture as above. Stuff cooked shells with beef mixture. Arrange shells in dish; top with remaining sauce. Cook, covered, 10 to 12 minutes or until heated through. Rotate dish halfway through cooking time. Top with remaining cheese and onions; cook, uncovered, 1 minute or until cheese melts. Let stand 5 minutes.

CHEESY BARBECUE BEEF

Ready to bake in just 10 easy minutes

1 pound ground beef
½ cup chopped green
pepper
1 can (12 ounces) whole kernel
corn, drained
1 cup barbecue sauce

1 tablespoon chili powder
1 can (2.8 ounces) Durkee
French Fried Onions
1 jar (8 ounces) pasteurized
processed cheese spread

Preheat oven to 350°. In large skillet, brown ground beef; drain. Add green pepper and cook until tender-crisp. Stir in corn, barbecue sauce, chili powder and ½ *can* French Fried Onions. Pour *half* the meat mixture into 1½-quart casserole; cover with *half* the cheese spread. Repeat layers. Bake, uncovered, at 350° for 20 to 25 minutes or until heated through. Top with remaining onions; bake, uncovered, 5 minutes or until onions are golden brown. Serve over buns, corn bread or rice if desired.   *Makes 4 servings*

MICROWAVE DIRECTIONS: Crumble ground beef into 1½-quart microwave-safe casserole; add green pepper. Cook, covered, on HIGH 4 to 6 minutes or until beef is cooked. Stir beef halfway through cooking time. Drain well. Stir in corn, barbecue sauce, chili powder, ½ *can* onions and the cheese spread. Cook, covered, 10 to 12 minutes or until heated through, stirring beef mixture halfway through cooking time. Stir casserole and top with remaining onions; cook, uncovered, 1 minute. Let stand 5 minutes.

HEARTY BEEF 'N VEGETABLES

Ready to bake in just 15 easy minutes

4 cups frozen potato rounds
1 pound ground beef
1 package (10 ounces) frozen
chopped broccoli, thawed
and drained
1 can (2.8 ounces) Durkee
French Fried Onions
1 medium tomato, chopped
(optional)

1 can (10¾ ounces) condensed
cream of celery soup
⅓ cup milk
1 cup (4 ounces) shredded
Cheddar cheese
¼ teaspoon garlic powder
⅛ teaspoon pepper

Preheat oven to 400°. Arrange frozen potatoes in bottom and up sides of 8×12-inch baking dish to form a shell. Bake, uncovered, at 400° for 10 minutes. In medium skillet, brown ground beef, leaving in large chunks; drain well. Layer beef, broccoli, ½ *can* French Fried Onions and the tomato in potato shell. In small bowl, combine

(continued)

Hearty Beef 'n Vegetables

soup, milk, ½ *cup* cheese and the seasonings; pour evenly over beef mixture. Bake, covered, at 400° for 20 minutes or until heated through. Top with remaining cheese and onions; bake, uncovered, 1 to 3 minutes or until onions are golden brown.

Makes 4 to 6 servings

MICROWAVE DIRECTIONS: In 8×12-inch microwave-safe dish, arrange potatoes as above; set aside. Crumble ground beef into large microwave-safe bowl. Cook, covered, on HIGH 4 to 6 minutes or until beef is cooked. Stir beef halfway through cooking time. Drain well. Stir in broccoli, ½ *can* onions, the soup, milk, ½ *cup* cheese and the seasonings. Cook, covered, 6 minutes, stirring beef mixture halfway through cooking time. Stir tomato into beef mixture; spoon into potato shell. Cook, covered, 8 minutes or until heated through. Rotate dish halfway through cooking time. Top with remaining cheese and onions; cook, uncovered, 1 minute or until cheese melts. Let stand 5 minutes.

PRONTO PORK & HAM

SAUSAGE-CHICKEN CREOLE

Ready to bake in just 15 easy minutes

1 can (14½ ounces) whole tomatoes, undrained and cut up
½ cup uncooked regular rice
½ cup hot water
2 teaspoons Durkee RedHot Cayenne Pepper Sauce
¼ teaspoon garlic powder
¼ teaspoon dried oregano, crumbled

1 bag (16 ounces) frozen vegetable combination (broccoli, corn, red pepper), thawed and drained
1 can (2.8 ounces) Durkee French Fried Onions
4 chicken thighs, skinned
½ pound link Italian sausage, quartered and cooked*
1 can (8 ounces) tomato sauce

Preheat oven to 375°. In 8×12-inch baking dish, combine tomatoes, uncooked rice, hot water, cayenne pepper sauce and seasonings. Bake, covered, at 375° for 10 minutes. Stir vegetables and ½ *can* French Fried Onions into rice mixture; top with chicken and cooked sausage. Pour tomato sauce over chicken and sausage. Bake, covered, at 375° for 40 minutes or until chicken is done. Top chicken with remaining onions; bake, uncovered, 3 minutes or until onions are golden brown.   *Makes 4 servings*

*To cook sausage, simmer in water to cover until done. Or, place in microwave-safe dish and cook, covered, on HIGH 3 minutes or until done.

MAKE-AHEAD BRUNCH BAKE

Refrigerate overnight; bake next day ━━━━━━━━━━

1 pound bulk pork
    sausage
6 eggs, beaten
2 cups light cream or half-and-
    half
½ teaspoon salt

1 teaspoon ground mustard
1 cup (4 ounces) shredded
    Cheddar cheese
1 can (2.8 ounces) Durkee
    French Fried Onions

Crumble sausage into large skillet. Cook over medium-high heat until browned; drain well. Stir in eggs, cream, salt, mustard, ½ *cup* cheese and ½ *can* French Fried Onions; mix well. Pour into greased 8×12-inch baking dish. Refrigerate, covered, 8 hours or overnight. Bake, uncovered, at 350° for 45 minutes or until knife inserted in center comes out clean. Top with remaining cheese and onions; bake, uncovered, 5 minutes or until onions are golden brown. Let stand 15 minutes before serving.   *Makes 6 servings*

MICROWAVE DIRECTIONS: Crumble sausage into 8×12-inch microwave-safe dish. Cook, covered, on HIGH 4 to 6 minutes or until sausage is cooked. Stir sausage halfway through cooking time. Drain well. Stir in ingredients and refrigerate as above. Cook, covered, 10 to 15 minutes or until center is firm. Stir egg mixture halfway through cooking time. Top with remaining cheese and onions; cook, uncovered, 1 minute or until cheese melts. Let stand 5 minutes.

PORK CHOPS O'BRIEN

Ready to bake in just 15 easy minutes ━━━━━━━━━━

1 tablespoon vegetable oil
6 pork chops, ½ to ¾ inch
    thick
    Seasoned salt
1 can (10¾ ounces) condensed
    cream of celery soup
½ cup milk
½ cup sour cream
¼ teaspoon pepper

1 bag (24 ounces) frozen
    O'Brien or hash brown
    potatoes, thawed
1 cup (4 ounces) shredded
    Cheddar cheese
1 can (2.8 ounces) Durkee
    French Fried Onions

Preheat oven to 350°. In large skillet, heat oil. Brown pork chops on both sides; drain. Sprinkle chops with seasoned salt; set aside. In large bowl, combine soup, milk, sour cream, pepper and ½ teaspoon seasoned salt. Stir in potatoes, ½ *cup* cheese and ½ *can* French Fried

(continued)

Pork Chops O'Brien

Onions. Spoon mixture into 9×13-inch baking dish; arrange pork chops on top. Bake, covered, at 350° for 35 to 40 minutes or until pork chops are done. Top chops with remaining cheese and onions; bake, uncovered, 5 minutes or until onions are golden brown.

Makes 6 servings

MICROWAVE DIRECTIONS: Omit oil. Prepare soup-potato mixture as above; spoon into 8×12-inch microwave-safe dish. Cook, covered, on HIGH 5 minutes. Stir well. Arrange *unbrowned* pork chops on top with meatiest parts toward edges of dish. Cook, covered, on MEDIUM (50-60%) 15 minutes. Turn chops over; sprinkle with seasoned salt. Stir potatoes and rotate dish. Cook, covered, on MEDIUM 12 to 15 minutes or until pork chops are done. Top chops with remaining cheese and onions; cook, uncovered, on HIGH 1 minute or until cheese melts. Let stand 5 minutes.

SAUCY PORK & CRANBERRY BAKE

Ready to bake in just 10 easy minutes

1 tablespoon vegetable oil
4 pork steaks, thinly sliced
    (about 3 pounds)
1 can (16 ounces) cranberry
    sauce with whole berries
½ cup ketchup
⅛ teaspoon ground
    allspice

1 bag (16 ounces) frozen sliced
    carrots, thawed and drained
1 can (8 ounces) pineapple
    chunks, drained
1 can (2.8 ounces) Durkee
    French Fried Onions

Preheat oven to 375°. In medium skillet, heat oil. Brown pork steaks on both sides. Remove steaks and drain fat from skillet. In same skillet, combine cranberries, ketchup and allspice; bring to a boil. Reduce heat and simmer 1 minute, stirring frequently. In 9 × 13-inch baking dish, combine carrots, pineapple and *½ can* French Fried Onions. Spoon *1 cup* cranberry-ketchup sauce over carrot mixture; top with steaks. Spoon *½ cup* sauce over steaks. Bake, covered, at 375° for 35 to 40 minutes or until pork steaks are done. Top steaks with remaining sauce and onions; bake, uncovered, 3 minutes or until onions are golden brown.   *Makes 4 to 6 servings*

PASTRY-WRAPPED KRAUT & FRANKS

Ready to bake in just 10 easy minutes

1 package (8 ounces)
    refrigerated crescent rolls
1 can (16 ounces) sauerkraut,
    drained
1 cup (4 ounces) shredded
    Swiss cheese

1 can (2.8 ounces) Durkee
    French Fried Onions
½ teaspoon caraway seed
    (optional)
1 pound frankfurters, cut into
    thirds

Preheat oven to 375°. Separate crescent dough into 8 triangles. In greased 9-inch pie plate, arrange triangles spoke-fashion so pointed tips hang over rim of plate about 3 inches. (Center of dish will not be covered with dough.) Set aside. In medium bowl, combine sauerkraut, *½ cup* cheese, *½ can* French Fried Onions and the caraway seeds. Spoon sauerkraut mixture evenly into pie plate; top with frankfurters. Bring points of dough over filling; pinch points together to seal. Bake, uncovered, at 375° for 40 to 45 minutes or until heated through. (If crust browns too quickly, cover during last 15 minutes of baking.) Top crust with remaining cheese and onions; bake, uncovered, 3 minutes or until onions are golden brown.
Makes 4 to 6 servings

HAM STARBURST CASSEROLE

Ready to bake in just 7 easy minutes

1 can (10¾ ounces) condensed
   cream of potato soup
¾ cup sour cream
1 can (16 ounces) sliced
   potatoes, drained
1 package (10 ounces) frozen
   peas, thawed and drained

1 can (2.8 ounces) Durkee
   French Fried Onions
2 tablespoons diced pimiento
   (optional)
8 to 12 ounces cooked ham or
   turkey ham, unsliced

Preheat oven to 350°. In medium bowl, combine soup, sour cream, potatoes, peas, ½ *can* French Fried Onions and the pimiento; stir well. Spoon into 10-inch round baking dish. Cut ham into 3 thick slices; cut each slice crosswise into halves. Press ham slices into potato mixture, rounded-side up in spoke-fashion, to form a starburst. Bake, covered, at 350° for 30 minutes or until heated through. Top with remaining onions; bake, uncovered, 5 minutes or until onions are golden brown. *Makes 4 servings*

SAVORY PORK CHOP SUPPER

Ready to bake in just 15 easy minutes

6 medium potatoes, thinly
   sliced (about 5 cups)
1 can (2.8 ounces) Durkee
   French Fried Onions
1 jar (2 ounces) sliced
   mushrooms, drained
2 tablespoons butter or
   margarine
¼ cup soy sauce

1½ teaspoons ground mustard
½ teaspoon Durkee RedHot
   Cayenne Pepper Sauce
⅛ teaspoon garlic powder
1 tablespoon vegetable oil
6 pork chops, ½ to ¾ inch
   thick

Preheat oven to 350°. In 8×12-inch baking dish, layer *half* the potatoes and ½ *can* French Fried Onions. Top with mushrooms and remaining potatoes. In small saucepan, melt butter; stir in soy sauce, mustard, cayenne pepper sauce and garlic powder. Brush *half* the soy sauce mixture over potatoes. In large skillet, heat oil. Brown pork chops on both sides; drain. Arrange chops over potatoes and brush with remaining soy sauce mixture. Bake, covered, at 350° for 1 hour. Bake, uncovered, 15 minutes or until pork chops and potatoes are done. Top chops with remaining onions; bake, uncovered, 5 minutes or until onions are golden brown. *Makes 4 to 6 servings*

HAM & PASTA ROLL-UPS

Ready to bake in just 20 easy minutes —————

6 lasagna noodles, cooked in
    unsalted water and drained
1 can (10¾ ounces) condensed
    cream of celery soup
1 tablespoon Dijon-style or
    prepared mustard
1 cup milk
1 cup (4 ounces) shredded
    Swiss cheese

1 package (10 ounces) frozen
    chopped spinach, thawed
    and well drained
⅓ cup (about 1½ ounces) grated
    Parmesan cheese
1 egg
1 can (2.8 ounces) Durkee
    French Fried Onions
6 thin slices deli ham (about
    ½ pound)

Preheat oven to 350°. Place hot noodles under cold running water until cool enough to handle; drain and set aside. In medium bowl, combine soup, mustard, milk and ½ *cup* Swiss cheese; pour *half* the soup mixture into 10-inch round or 8×12-inch baking dish. In small bowl, combine spinach, Parmesan cheese, egg and ½ *can* French Fried Onions; stir until well blended. Fold each ham slice in half lengthwise and place on one end of cooled lasagna noodle. Top ham with ¼ cup spinach mixture. Roll up noodles tightly, jelly-roll style. With sharp knife, cut roll-ups into halves. Arrange in dish, ruffled-side up. Pour remaining soup mixture over roll-ups. Bake, covered, at 350° for 30 minutes or until heated through. Top with remaining Swiss cheese and onions; bake, uncovered, 5 minutes or until onions are golden brown.   *Makes 6 servings*

MICROWAVE DIRECTIONS: Prepare soup and spinach mixtures as above. Pour *half* the soup mixture into 8×12-inch microwave-safe dish. Assemble roll-ups and place in dish as above; top with remaining soup mixture. Cook, covered, on HIGH 10 to 12 minutes or until heated through. Rotate dish halfway through cooking time. Top with remaining Swiss cheese and onions; cook, uncovered, 1 minute or until cheese melts. Let stand 5 minutes.

STUFFED FRANKS 'N TATERS

Ready to bake in just 5 easy minutes —————

4 cups frozen hash brown
    potatoes, thawed
1 can (10¾ ounces) condensed
    cream of celery soup
1 cup (4 ounces) shredded
    Cheddar cheese
1 cup sour cream

1 can (2.8 ounces) Durkee
    French Fried Onions
½ teaspoon salt
¼ teaspoon pepper
6 frankfurters

(continued)

Stuffed Franks 'n Taters

Preheat oven to 400°. In large bowl, combine potatoes, soup, ½ *cup* cheese, the sour cream, ½ *can* French Fried Onions and the seasonings. Spread potato mixture in 8×12-inch baking dish. Split frankfurters lengthwise almost into halves. Arrange frankfurters, split-side up, along center of casserole. Bake, covered, at 400° for 30 minutes or until heated through. Fill frankfurters with remaining cheese and onions; bake, uncovered, 1 to 3 minutes or until onions are golden brown.   *Makes 6 servings*

MICROWAVE DIRECTIONS: Prepare potato mixture as above; spread in 8×12-inch microwave-safe dish. Cook, covered, on HIGH 8 minutes; stir potato mixture halfway through cooking time. Split frankfurters and arrange on potatoes as above. Cook, covered, 4 to 6 minutes or until frankfurters are heated through. Rotate dish halfway through cooking time. Fill frankfurters with remaining cheese and onions; cook, uncovered, 1 minute or until cheese melts. Let stand 5 minutes.

SAUSAGE SUCCOTASH

Ready to bake in just 15 easy minutes

1 pound kielbasa, cut into
½-inch slices and cooked*
1 package (10 ounces) frozen
lima beans, thawed and
drained
2 cups frozen hash brown
potatoes, thawed
1 cup (4 ounces) shredded
Cheddar cheese

1 can (2.8 ounces) Durkee
French Fried Onions
1 can (10¾ ounces) condensed
cream of potato soup
¾ cup milk
1 can (8 ounces) creamed corn
¼ teaspoon seasoned salt

Preheat oven to 350°. In large bowl, combine sausage, lima beans,
potatoes, *½ cup* cheese, *½ can* French Fried Onions, the soup, milk,
corn and seasoned salt. Pour into 8 × 12-inch baking dish. Bake,
covered, at 350° for 30 minutes or until heated through. Top with
remaining cheese and onions; bake, uncovered, 5 minutes or until
onions are golden brown.   *Makes 4 to 6 servings*

*To cook kielbasa, simmer in water to cover until heated through.
Or, place in microwave-safe dish and cook, covered, on HIGH 3
minutes or until heated through.

MICROWAVE DIRECTIONS: Prepare sausage mixture as above;
pour into 8 × 12-inch microwave-safe dish. Cook, covered, on HIGH
5 to 8 minutes or until heated through. Stir casserole halfway
through cooking time. Top with remaining cheese and onions; cook,
uncovered, 1 minute or until cheese melts. Let stand 5 minutes.

HAM & MACARONI TWISTS

Ready to bake in just 7 easy minutes

2 cups rotini or elbow
macaroni, cooked in
unsalted water and drained
1½ cups (8 ounces) cubed cooked
ham
1 can (2.8 ounces) Durkee
French Fried Onions
1 package (10 ounces) frozen
broccoli spears,* thawed
and drained

1 cup milk
1 can (10¾ ounces) condensed
cream of celery soup
1 cup (4 ounces) shredded
Cheddar cheese
¼ teaspoon garlic powder
¼ teaspoon pepper

*1 small head fresh broccoli (about ½ pound) may be substituted for
frozen spears. Divide into spears and cook 3 to 4 minutes before
using.
(continued)

Ham & Macaroni Twists

Preheat oven to 350°. In 8×12-inch baking dish, combine hot macaroni, ham and ½ *can* French Fried Onions. Divide broccoli spears into 6 small bunches. Arrange bunches of spears down center of dish, alternating direction of flowerets. In small bowl, combine milk, soup, ½ *cup* cheese and the seasonings; pour over casserole. Bake, covered, at 350° for 30 minutes or until heated through. Top with remaining cheese and sprinkle onions down center; bake, uncovered, 5 minutes or until onions are golden brown.

Makes 4 to 6 servings

MICROWAVE DIRECTIONS: In 8×12-inch microwave-safe dish, prepare macaroni mixture and arrange broccoli spears as above. Prepare soup mixture as above; pour over casserole. Cook, covered, on HIGH 8 minutes or until broccoli is done. Rotate dish halfway through cooking time. Top with remaining cheese and onions as above; cook, uncovered, 1 minute or until cheese melts. Let stand 5 minutes.

PORK STRIPS FLORENTINE

Ready to bake in just 5 easy minutes

1 pound boneless pork strips
1 package (6 ounces) seasoned
  long grain and wild
  rice mix
1⅔ cups hot water
1 can (2.8 ounces) Durkee
  French Fried Onions
¼ teaspoon garlic
  powder

1 package (10 ounces) frozen
  chopped spinach, thawed
  and well drained
2 tablespoons diced pimiento
  (optional)
½ cup (2 ounces) shredded
  Swiss cheese

Preheat oven to 375°. In 8×12-inch baking dish, combine pork strips, uncooked rice, contents of rice seasoning packet, hot water, *½ can* French Fried Onions and garlic powder. Bake, covered, at 375° for 30 minutes. Stir spinach and pimiento into meat mixture. Bake, covered, 10 minutes or until pork and rice are done. Top with cheese and remaining onions; bake, uncovered, 3 minutes or until onions are golden brown. *Makes 4 servings*

HAM-STUFFED PEPPERS

Ready to bake in just 15 easy minutes

1½ cups cooked unsalted regular
  rice (½ cup uncooked)
1 cup (5 ounces) diced cooked
  ham
1 can (16 ounces) whole kernel
  corn, drained
1 jar (15½ ounces) spaghetti
  sauce
1 cup (4 ounces) shredded
  Cheddar cheese

1 can (2.8 ounces) Durkee
  French Fried Onions
¼ teaspoon seasoned salt
¼ teaspoon black pepper
4 medium green peppers, cut
  into halves lengthwise and
  seeded
¼ cup water

Preheat oven to 350°. To hot rice in saucepan, add ham, corn, *1 cup* spaghetti sauce, *½ cup* cheese, *½ can* French Fried Onions and the seasonings; stir well. Spoon rice filling into green pepper halves. Arrange stuffed peppers in 8×12-inch baking dish. In small bowl, combine remaining spaghetti sauce and the water; pour over peppers. Bake, covered, at 350° for 30 minutes or until peppers are done. Top with remaining cheese and onions; bake, uncovered, 5 minutes or until onions are golden brown. *Makes 4 servings*

SAUSAGE POPOVER BAKE

Ready to bake in just 15 easy minutes ——————————

½ pound bulk Italian sausage
1 can (12 ounces) whole kernel
corn with sweet peppers,
drained
1 can (4 ounces) mushroom
stems and pieces, drained
1 cup (4 ounces) shredded
Monterey Jack cheese

1 can (2.8 ounces) Durkee
French Fried Onions
2 eggs, slightly beaten
1 cup all-purpose flour
1 cup milk
1 tablespoon vegetable oil
½ teaspoon chili powder

Preheat oven to 400°. Crumble sausage into large skillet. Cook over medium-high heat until browned; drain well. Stir in corn, mushrooms, ½ cup cheese and ½ can French Fried Onions. Spoon sausage mixture into *well-greased* (do not use vegetable cooking spray) 9-inch square baking dish. In small bowl, combine eggs, flour, milk, oil and chili powder; beat until smooth and well blended. Pour over sausage mixture. Bake, uncovered, at 400° for 30 minutes or until top is golden brown. Top with remaining cheese and onions; bake, uncovered, 1 to 3 minutes or until onions are golden brown.

Makes 4 to 6 servings

PORK CHOPS MADRID

Ready to bake in just 12 easy minutes ——————————

1 tablespoon vegetable oil
4 pork chops, ½ to ¾ inch
thick
½ teaspoon seasoned salt
1 can (14½ ounces) whole
tomatoes, undrained and
cut up

1 can (16 ounces) whole kernel
corn, drained
½ cup uncooked regular rice
½ cup water
1½ cup chopped green pepper
1 teaspoon Durkee RedHot
Cayenne Pepper Sauce
1 can (2.8 ounces) Durkee
French Fried Onions

Preheat oven to 350°. In large skillet, heat oil. Brown pork chops on both sides; drain well. Sprinkle chops with seasoned salt; set aside. In same skillet, combine tomatoes, corn, uncooked rice, water, green pepper and cayenne pepper sauce; bring to a boil. Remove from heat and stir in ½ can French Fried Onions. Spoon rice mixture into 8×12-inch baking dish; arrange pork chops on top. Bake, covered, at 350° for 35 to 40 minutes or until rice and pork chops are done. Top pork chops with remaining onions; bake, uncovered, 5 minutes or until onions are golden brown.

Makes 4 servings

BAKED HAM & CHEESE MONTE CRISTO

Ready to bake in just 15 easy minutes ───────

6 slices bread
2 cups (8 ounces) shredded
   Cheddar cheese
1 can (2.8 ounces) Durkee
   French Fried Onions
1 package (10 ounces) frozen
   broccoli spears, thawed,
   drained and cut into 1-inch
   pieces

2 cups (10 ounces) cubed
   cooked ham
5 eggs
2 cups milk
½ teaspoon ground mustard
½ teaspoon seasoned salt
¼ teaspoon coarsely ground
   black pepper

Preheat oven to 325°. Cut *3* bread slices into cubes; place in greased
8 × 12-inch baking dish. Top bread with *1 cup* cheese, *½ can* French
Fried Onions, the broccoli and ham. Cut remaining bread slices
diagonally into halves. Arrange bread halves down center of
casserole, overlapping slightly, crusted points all in 1 direction. In
medium bowl, beat eggs, milk and seasonings; pour evenly over
casserole. Bake, uncovered, at 325° for 1 hour or until center is set.
Top with remaining cheese and onions; bake, uncovered, 5 minutes
or until onions are golden brown. Let stand 10 minutes before
serving.   *Makes 6 to 8 servings*

CHEESY PORK CHOPS 'N POTATOES

Ready to bake in just 15 easy minutes ───────

1 jar (8 ounces) pasteurized
   processed cheese spread
1 tablespoon vegetable oil
6 thin pork chops, ¼ to ½ inch
   thick
   Seasoned salt
½ cup milk

4 cups frozen cottage fries
1 can (2.8 ounces) Durkee
   French Fried Onions
1 package (10 ounces) frozen
   broccoli spears,* thawed
   and drained

* 1 small head fresh broccoli (about ½ pound) may be substituted for
frozen spears. Divide into spears and cook 3 to 4 minutes before
using.

Preheat oven to 350°. Spoon cheese spread into 8 × 12-inch baking
dish; place in oven just until cheese melts, 5 minutes. Meanwhile,
in large skillet, heat oil. Brown pork chops on both sides; drain.
Sprinkle chops with seasoned salt; set aside. Using fork, stir milk
into melted cheese until well blended. Stir cottage fries and *½ can*
French Fried Onions into cheese mixture. Divide broccoli spears into

(continued)

Cheesy Pork Chops 'n Potatoes

6 small bunches. Arrange bunches of spears over potato mixture with flowerets around edges of dish. Arrange chops over broccoli *stalks*. Bake, covered, at 350° for 35 to 40 minutes or until pork chops are done. Top chops with remaining onions; bake, uncovered, 5 minutes or until onions are golden brown.

Makes 4 to 6 servings

MICROWAVE DIRECTIONS: Omit oil. Reduce milk to ¼ cup. In 8×12-inch microwave-safe dish, place cheese spread and milk. Cook, covered, on HIGH 3 minutes; stir to blend. Stir in cottage fries and ½ *can* onions. Cook, covered, 5 minutes; stir. Top with broccoli spears as above. Arrange *unbrowned* pork chops over broccoli *stalks* with meatiest parts toward edges of dish. Cook, covered, on MEDIUM (50-60%) 24 to 30 minutes or until pork chops are done. Turn chops over, sprinkle with seasoned salt and rotate dish halfway through cooking time. Top with remaining onions; cook, uncovered, on HIGH 1 minute. Let stand 5 minutes.

EXPRESS VEGGIES, PASTA & MORE

CHEESY PASTA SWIRLS

Ready to bake in just 15 easy minutes

4 ounces fettucine, cooked in unsalted water and drained

1 bag (16 ounces) frozen vegetable combination (peas, carrots, cauliflower), thawed and drained

1 cup (4 ounces) shredded mozzarella cheese

½ cup (2 ounces) cubed provolone cheese

1 can (2.8 ounces) Durkee French Fried Onions

1 can (10¾ ounces) condensed cream of mushroom soup

¾ cup milk

½ teaspoon garlic salt

⅓ cup (about 1½ ounces) grated Parmesan cheese

Preheat oven to 350°. In 8×12-inch baking dish, combine vegetables, mozzarella, provolone and ½ can French Fried Onions. Twirl a few strands of hot fettucine around long-tined fork to form a pasta swirl. Remove pasta swirl from fork; stand upright on top of vegetable mixture. Repeat process to form 5 more swirls. In medium bowl, stir together soup, milk and garlic salt; pour over pasta swirls and vegetable mixture. Bake, loosely covered, at 350° for 30 minutes or until vegetables are done. Top pasta swirls with Parmesan cheese; sprinkle remaining onions around swirls. Bake, uncovered, 5 minutes or until onions are golden brown.   *Makes 6 servings*

MICROWAVE DIRECTIONS: In 8×12-inch microwave-safe dish, prepare vegetable mixture as above. Form pasta swirls and place on vegetables as above. Prepare soup mixture as above; pour over pasta and vegetables. Cook, loosely covered, on HIGH 14 to 16 minutes or until vegetables are done. Rotate dish halfway through cooking time. Top pasta swirls with Parmesan cheese and remaining onions as above; cook, uncovered, 1 minute. Let stand 5 minutes.

CASSEROLE PRIMAVERA

Ready to bake in just 15 easy minutes _____

2 cups (4 ounces) spinach
  noodles
4 ounces linguini
½ cup thinly sliced zucchini
1 can (2.8 ounces) Durkee
  French Fried Onions
1 cup (4 ounces) shredded
  provolone cheese
½ cup (2 ounces) grated
  Parmesan cheese

2 tablespoons all-purpose flour
1 teaspoon garlic salt
½ teaspoon Italian seasoning
2½ cups milk
1 cup chopped tomato
⅓ cup sliced pitted ripe olives

Preheat oven to 325°. In large saucepan, cook noodles and linguini according to package directions, omitting salt. Add zucchini during last 2 minutes of cooking. Drain. Return pasta and zucchini to saucepan. Toss lightly with ½ *can* French Fried Onions, the cheeses, flour, seasonings, milk, tomato and olives. Pour into 8×12-inch baking dish. Bake, covered, at 325° for 25 minutes or until heated through. Stir to blend sauce and noodles. Top with remaining onions; bake, uncovered, 5 minutes or until onions are golden brown.   *Makes 6 main-dish servings*

MICROWAVE DIRECTIONS: Prepare pasta mixture as above; pour into 8×12-inch microwave-safe dish. Cook, covered, on HIGH 12 to 14 minutes or until heated through. Stir pasta mixture halfway through cooking time. Top with remaining onions; cook, uncovered, 1 minute. Let stand 5 minutes.

VEGETABLE SUNBURST

Ready to bake in just 15 easy minutes _____

3 medium carrots, thinly sliced
  (about 3 cups)
3 small zucchini,
  thinly sliced
  (about 3 cups)
1 cup (4 ounces) shredded
  Cheddar cheese
1 can (2.8 ounces) Durkee
  French Fried Onions

1 can (10¾ ounces) condensed
  cream of celery soup
¼ cup milk
½ teaspoon seasoned salt
¼ teaspoon garlic powder
¼ teaspoon dried oregano
  leaves, crumbled

Preheat oven to 350°. In medium saucepan, cook carrots in boiling water to cover just until tender-crisp. Place hot carrots under cold running water until cool enough to handle; drain. In 1½-quart casserole, arrange *half* the carrots around edge of dish; place *half* the

(continued)

Vegetable Sunburst

zucchini in center. Sprinkle ½ *cup* cheese and ½ *can* French Fried Onions over vegetables. In small bowl, combine soup, milk and seasonings. Pour *half* the soup mixture over onions. Arrange remaining zucchini around edge of casserole and remaining carrots in center. Pour remaining soup mixture over vegetables. Bake, covered, at 350° for 30 minutes or until vegetables are tender. Top with remaining cheese and onions; bake, uncovered, 5 minutes or until onions are golden brown.   *Makes 4 to 6 servings*

MICROWAVE DIRECTIONS: Place carrots and ½ cup water in medium microwave-safe bowl; cook on HIGH 5 to 7 minutes or until carrots are tender-crisp. Stir carrots halfway through cooking time. Drain. Prepare soup mixture as above. In 1½-quart microwave-safe casserole, layer vegetables, cheese, onions and soup mixture as above. Cook, covered, 8 to 10 minutes or until vegetables are tender. Rotate dish halfway through cooking time. Top with remaining cheese and onions; cook, uncovered, 1 minute or until cheese melts. Let stand 5 minutes.

HOT GERMAN-STYLE POTATO SALAD

Ready to bake in just 12 easy minutes

5 slices bacon
1 medium green or red pepper,
  cut into ½-inch chunks
⅓ cup water
3 tablespoons cider vinegar
2 teaspoons sugar
2 teaspoons cornstarch

¼ teaspoon salt
⅛ teaspoon black pepper
2 cans (16 ounces *each*) sliced
  potatoes, drained
1 can (2.8 ounces) Durkee
  French Fried Onions

Preheat oven to 375°. In large skillet, fry bacon until crisp. Remove from skillet; crumble and set aside. Drain all but about 2 tablespoons drippings from skillet; add green pepper and cook until tender-crisp. Stir in water, vinegar, sugar, cornstarch and seasonings. Simmer, uncovered, until thickened. Gently stir in potatoes, crumbled bacon and ½ *can* French Fried Onions; spoon into 1½-quart casserole. Bake, covered, at 375° for 35 minutes or until heated through. Top with remaining onions; bake, uncovered, 3 minutes or until onions are golden brown.   *Makes 4 servings*

MONTEREY SPAGHETTI CASSEROLE

Ready to bake in just 7 easy minutes

4 ounces spaghetti, cooked in
  unsalted water and
  drained
1 egg, beaten
1 cup sour cream
¼ cup (1 ounce) grated
  Parmesan cheese
¼ teaspoon garlic powder

2 cups (8 ounces) shredded
  Monterey Jack cheese
1 package (10 ounces) frozen
  chopped spinach, thawed
  and well drained
1 can (2.8 ounces) Durkee
  French Fried Onions

Preheat oven to 350°. In medium bowl, combine egg, sour cream, Parmesan cheese and garlic powder. Stir in Monterey Jack cheese, hot spaghetti, spinach and ½ *can* French Fried Onions. Pour into 8-inch square baking dish. Bake, covered, at 350° for 30 minutes or until heated through. Top with remaining onions; bake, uncovered, 5 minutes or until onions are golden brown.

Makes 4 main-dish servings

MICROWAVE DIRECTIONS: Prepare spaghetti mixture as above; pour into 8-inch square microwave-safe dish. Cook, covered, on HIGH 8 to 10 minutes or until heated through. Stir spaghetti halfway through cooking time. Top with remaining onions; cook, uncovered, 1 minute. Let stand 5 minutes.

BUFFET BEAN BAKE

Ready to bake in just 17 easy minutes

6 slices bacon
1 cup packed brown sugar
½ cup vinegar
½ teaspoon salt
1 tablespoon prepared mustard
1 can (16 ounces) butter beans, drained
1 can (16 ounces) French-style green beans, drained

1 can (16 ounces) pork and beans, drained
1 can (16 ounces) lima beans, drained
1 can (15½ ounces) yellow wax beans, drained
1 can (15 ounces) kidney beans, drained
1 can (2.8 ounces) Durkee French Fried Onions

Preheat oven to 350°. In medium skillet, fry bacon until crisp. Remove from skillet; crumble and set aside. Drain all but about 2 tablespoons drippings from skillet; add sugar, vinegar, salt and mustard. Simmer, uncovered, 10 minutes. In large bowl, combine drained beans, *½ can* French Fried Onions and hot sugar mixture. Spoon bean mixture into 9×13-inch baking dish. Bake, covered, at 350° for 30 minutes or until heated through. Top with crumbled bacon and remaining onions; bake, uncovered, 5 minutes or until onions are golden brown. *Makes 12 to 14 servings*

SPINACH-ONION STUFFING BALLS

Ready to bake in just 7 easy minutes

1¼ cups water
3 cups seasoned stuffing croutons *
1 package (10 ounces) frozen chopped spinach, thawed and well drained

1 can (2.8 ounces) Durkee French Fried Onions
½ cup (2 ounces) shredded Swiss cheese

Preheat oven to 350°. In large saucepan, heat *1 cup* water to a boil. Add stuffing croutons; stir to moisten. Add spinach and *⅔ can* French Fried Onions; mix until thoroughly combined. Using ½ cup measure, shape stuffing into 6 equal balls; place in 10-inch round baking dish. Add remaining water to dish. Bake, covered, at 350° for 30 minutes or until heated through. Top with cheese and remaining onions; bake, uncovered, 5 minutes or until onions are golden brown. *Makes 6 servings*

*1 package (6 ounces) stuffing mix may be substituted for croutons and 1 cup water. Prepare according to package directions, omitting butter; stir in spinach and onions as above.

HARVEST VEGETABLE SCALLOP

Ready to bake in just 15 easy minutes

4 medium carrots, thinly sliced
(about 2 cups)
1 package (10 ounces) frozen
chopped broccoli, thawed
and drained
1 can (2.8 ounces) Durkee
French Fried Onions
5 small red potatoes, sliced
⅛ inch thick
(about 2 cups)

1 jar (8 ounces) pasteurized
processed cheese spread
¼ cup milk
Pepper
Seasoned salt

Preheat oven to 375°. In 8×12-inch baking dish, combine carrots, broccoli and *½ can* French Fried Onions. Tuck potato slices into vegetable mixture at an angle. Dot vegetables evenly with cheese spread. Pour milk over vegetables; sprinkle with seasonings as desired. Bake, covered, at 375° for 30 minutes or until vegetables are tender. Top with remaining onions; bake, uncovered, 3 minutes or until onions are golden brown. *Makes 6 servings*

MICROWAVE DIRECTIONS: In 8×12-inch microwave-safe dish, prepare vegetables as above. Top with cheese spread, milk and seasonings as above. Cook, covered, on HIGH 12 to 14 minutes or until vegetables are tender. Rotate dish halfway through cooking time. Top with remaining onions; cook, uncovered, 1 minute. Let stand 5 minutes.

SWEET POTATO-CRANBERRY BAKE

Ready to bake in just 5 easy minutes

1 can (40 ounces) whole sweet
potatoes, drained
1 can (2.8 ounces) Durkee
French Fried Onions

2 cups fresh cranberries
2 tablespoons packed brown
sugar
⅓ cup honey

Preheat oven to 400°. In 1½-quart casserole, layer sweet potatoes, *½ can* French Fried Onions and *1 cup* cranberries. Sprinkle with brown sugar; drizzle with *half* the honey. Top with remaining cranberries and honey. Bake, covered, at 400° for 35 minutes or until heated through. Gently stir casserole. Top with remaining onions; bake, uncovered, 1 to 3 minutes or until onions are golden brown.

Makes 4 to 6 servings

Harvest Vegetable Scallop

OLD-FASHIONED STUFFING

Ready to bake in just 10 easy minutes ━━━━━━

½ cup butter or margarine
3 cups diced celery
1½ teaspoons poultry
   seasoning
¾ teaspoon seasoned salt
¼ teaspoon pepper
24 slices day-old bread, cut into
   cubes (about 3 quarts)

1 can (6 ounces) Durkee French
   Fried Onions
2 to 3 cups chicken broth

Preheat oven to 350°. In large saucepan, melt butter; add celery, seasonings, bread cubes and *all but ½ cup* of the French Fried Onions. Moisten with broth until well mixed. (Add more broth if moister stuffing is desired.) Place in 3-quart casserole. Bake, covered, at 350° for 25 minutes. Uncover and bake 10 minutes or until heated through and top is crusty. Top with remaining onions; bake, uncovered, 5 minutes or until onions are golden brown.

Makes about 6 cups stuffing

MICROWAVE DIRECTIONS: In 3-quart microwave-safe casserole, melt butter, uncovered, on HIGH 1 minute. Stir in ingredients as above. Cook, covered, 10 minutes or until heated through. Stir stuffing halfway through cooking time. Top with remaining onions; cook, uncovered, 1 minute. Let stand 5 minutes.

EASY SPINACH-ZUCCHINI PIE

Ready to bake in just 15 easy minutes ━━━━━━

1 to 2 medium zucchini (each
   about 8 inches long)
Hot water
2 packages (10 ounces *each*)
   frozen chopped spinach,
   thawed and well drained
½ cup sour cream
1 package (3 ounces) cream
   cheese, softened
¼ cup (1 ounce) grated
   Parmesan cheese

3 tablespoons dry bread crumbs
1 egg, slightly beaten
½ teaspoon garlic salt
½ teaspoon dried basil,
   crumbled
1 can (2.8 ounces) Durkee
   French Fried Onions
½ cup (2 ounces) shredded
   Cheddar cheese

Preheat oven to 375°. Using sharp knife, trim off 1 side of zucchini to form a straight edge. Starting at straight edge, cut zucchini lengthwise into eight thin strips (about ⅛ inch thick). Place zucchini strips in shallow dish filled with hot water about 3 minutes to soften; drain. In large bowl, using fork, thoroughly combine spinach,

(continued)

Easy Spinach-Zucchini Pie

sour cream, cream cheese, Parmesan cheese, bread crumbs, egg, seasonings and ⅔ *can* French Fried Onions. Line bottom and side of 9-inch pie plate or quiche dish with zucchini strips, allowing 3 inches of each strip to hang over edge. Spoon spinach mixture evenly into pie plate. Fold zucchini strips over spinach mixture, tucking ends into center of mixture. Cover pie plate with foil. Bake, covered, at 375° for 40 minutes or until zucchini is tender. Top center of pie with cheese and remaining onions; bake, uncovered, 3 minutes or until onions are golden brown.   *Makes 6 to 8 servings*

MICROWAVE DIRECTIONS: Cut zucchini into strips as above. Place zucchini strips in shallow microwave-safe dish and cook, covered, on HIGH 2 minutes or until softened; drain. Prepare spinach mixture as above. Line 9-inch microwave-safe pie plate with zucchini strips and fill as above. Cook, covered, 12 to 14 minutes or until zucchini is tender. Rotate dish halfway through cooking time. Top center of pie with cheese and remaining onions; cook, uncovered, 1 minute or until cheese melts. Let stand 5 minutes.

HOLIDAY STUFFING & POTATO BAKE

Ready to bake in just 15 easy minutes

1½ cups water
¼ cup butter or margarine
1 package (6 ounces) corn bread
  stuffing mix*
1 cup chopped apple
½ cup chopped celery

1 egg, beaten
1 can (2.8 ounces) Durkee
  French Fried Onions
3 cups hot mashed potatoes
1 cup (4 ounces) shredded
  Cheddar Cheese

Preheat oven to 350°. In large saucepan, heat water and butter until butter melts; remove from heat. Stir in both pouches of stuffing mix, apple, celery, egg and ½ can French Fried Onions; mix well. Set aside. To hot mashed potatoes, add ½ cup Cheddar cheese; stir. In greased 8×12-inch baking dish, make 4 alternating rows of potatoes and stuffing. Bake, covered, at 350° for 30 minutes or until heated through. Sprinkle remaining cheese and onions between each row of stuffing and potatoes; bake, uncovered, 5 minutes or until onions are golden brown. *Makes 4 to 6 servings*

*3 cups corn bread stuffing crumbs may be substituted for stuffing mix. Substitute 1 cup chicken broth for the water.

MICROWAVE DIRECTIONS: In medium microwave-safe bowl, place water and butter. Cook, covered, on HIGH 3 minutes or until butter melts. Stir in stuffing ingredients as above. Prepare potato mixture as above. In 8×12-inch microwave-safe dish, arrange stuffing and potatoes as above. Cook, covered, 8 to 10 minutes or until heated through. Rotate dish halfway through cooking time. Top with remaining cheese and onions as above; cook, uncovered, 1 minute or until cheese melts. Let stand 5 minutes.

CHUCK WAGON BEANS

Ready to bake in just 5 easy minutes

1 can (15 ounces) kidney beans,
  drained
1 can (16 ounces) butter beans
  or Great Northern beans,
  drained

1 cup barbecue sauce
1 can (2.8 ounces) Durkee
  French Fried Onions
4 slices uncooked bacon, diced

Preheat oven to 350°. In 1½-quart casserole, combine beans, barbecue sauce and ½ can French Fried Onions; top with bacon. Bake, covered, at 350° for 45 minutes or until heated through. Top with remaining onions; bake, uncovered, 5 minutes or until onions are golden brown. *Makes 4 to 6 servings*

DILLY VEGETABLE SHOW-OFF

Ready to bake in just 7 easy minutes

1 can (10¾ ounces) condensed cream of celery soup
½ cup sour cream
¼ cup milk
½ teaspoon dried dill weed, crumbled
1 can (2.8 ounces) Durkee French Fried Onions

1 bag (16 ounces) frozen broccoli cuts, thawed and drained
1 package (10 ounces) frozen cauliflower, thawed and drained
½ cup (2 ounces) shredded Cheddar cheese

Preheat oven to 375°. In small bowl, combine soup, sour cream, milk and dill weed. Pour *half* the soup mixture into 10-inch round baking dish; top with ½ *can* French Fried Onions. Arrange broccoli around edge of dish; place cauliflower in center. Pour remaining soup mixture over broccoli and cauliflower. Bake, covered, at 375° for 30 minutes or until heated through. Top with cheese and remaining onions; bake, uncovered, 3 minutes or until onions are golden brown.

Makes 6 servings

MICROWAVE DIRECTIONS: Prepare soup mixture as above; pour *half* into 10-inch round microwave-safe dish. Arrange vegetables in dish as above; top with remaining soup mixture. Cook, covered, on HIGH 10 to 12 minutes or until heated through. Rotate dish halfway through cooking time. Top with cheese and remaining onions; cook, uncovered, 1 minute or until cheese melts. Let stand 5 minutes.

BROCCOLI & EGG AU GRATIN

Ready to bake in just 5 easy minutes

1 can (10¾ ounces) condensed cream of celery soup
⅔ cup milk
2 packages (10 ounces *each*) frozen broccoli spears, thawed and drained

3 hard-cooked eggs, sliced
1 can (2.8 ounces) Durkee French Fried Onions
½ cup (2 ounces) shredded Swiss cheese

Preheat oven to 350°. In small bowl, combine soup and milk. In 8 × 12-inch baking dish, arrange broccoli spears down center of dish, alternating direction of flowerets. Layer eggs, ½ *can* French Fried Onions, the soup mixture and cheese over broccoli *stalks*. Bake, covered, at 350° for 25 minutes or until heated through. Top with remaining onions; bake, uncovered, 5 minutes or until onions are golden brown.

Makes 6 servings

ORIGINAL GREEN BEAN CASSEROLE ▶

Ready to bake in just 5 easy minutes

2 cans (16 ounces *each*) cut
    green beans, drained or
    2 packages (9 ounces *each*)
    frozen cut green beans,
    cooked and drained
¾ cup milk

1 can (10¾ ounces) condensed
    cream of mushroom soup
⅛ teaspoon pepper
1 can (2.8 ounces) Durkee
    French Fried Onions

Preheat oven to 350°. In medium bowl, combine beans, milk, soup, pepper and ½ *can* French Fried Onions; pour into 1½-quart casserole. Bake, uncovered, at 350° for 30 minutes or until heated through. Top with remaining onions; bake, uncovered, 5 minutes or until onions are golden brown.   *Makes 6 servings*

MICROWAVE DIRECTIONS: Prepare green bean mixture as above; pour into 1½-quart microwave-safe casserole. Cook, covered, on HIGH 8 to 10 minutes or until heated through. Stir beans halfway through cooking time. Top with remaining onions; cook, uncovered, 1 minute. Let stand 5 minutes.

SWISS VEGETABLE MEDLEY ▶

Ready to bake in just 5 easy minutes

1 bag (16 ounces) frozen
    vegetable combination
    (broccoli, carrots,
    cauliflower), thawed and
    drained
1 can (10¾ ounces) condensed
    cream of mushroom soup
1 cup (4 ounces) shredded
    Swiss cheese

⅓ cup sour cream
¼ teaspoon pepper
1 jar (4 ounces) diced pimiento,
    drained (optional)
1 can (2.8 ounces) Durkee
    French Fried Onions

Preheat oven to 350°. In large bowl, combine vegetables, soup, ½ *cup* cheese, the sour cream, pepper, pimiento and ½ *can* French Fried Onions. Pour into shallow 1-quart casserole. Bake, covered, at 350° for 30 minutes or until vegetables are done. Sprinkle remaining cheese and onions in diagonal rows across top; bake, uncovered, 5 minutes or until onions are golden brown.   *Makes 6 servings*

MICROWAVE DIRECTIONS: Prepare vegetable mixture as above; pour into shallow 1-quart microwave-safe casserole. Cook, covered, on HIGH 8 to 10 minutes or until vegetables are done. Stir vegetables halfway through cooking time. Top with remaining cheese and onions as above; cook, uncovered, 1 minute or until cheese melts. Let stand 5 minutes.

SIMPLY SPECIAL VEGETABLE PIE

Ready to bake in just 10 easy minutes

1 package (10 ounces) frozen
   chopped spinach, thawed
   and well drained
1 can (2.8 ounces) Durkee
   French Fried Onions
1 egg
½ teaspoon garlic salt
1 package (about 1⅛ ounces)
   cheese sauce mix

1 cup milk
1 bag (16 ounces) frozen
   vegetable combination
   (broccoli, carrots, red
   pepper, water chestnuts),
   thawed and drained

Preheat oven to 350°. In small bowl, combine spinach, *½ can* French Fried Onions, the egg and garlic salt; stir until well mixed. Using back of spoon, spread spinach mixture across bottom and up side of greased 9-inch pie plate to form a shell. In medium saucepan, prepare cheese sauce mix according to package directions using milk; stir in vegetables. Pour vegetable mixture into spinach shell. Bake, covered, at 350° for 30 minutes or until heated through. Top with remaining onions; bake, uncovered, 5 minutes or until onions are golden brown.   *Makes 6 servings*

MICROWAVE DIRECTIONS: In medium microwave-safe bowl, prepare cheese sauce mix according to package microwave directions using milk; stir vegetables into sauce. Prepare spinach mixture as above; spread in 9-inch microwave-safe pie plate as above. Pour vegetable mixture into spinach shell. Cook, loosely covered, 6 to 8 minutes or until vegetables are done. Rotate dish halfway through cooking time. Top with remaining onions; cook, uncovered, 1 minute. Let stand 5 minutes.

SAUCY GARDEN PATCH VEGETABLES

Ready to bake in just 7 easy minutes

1 can (11 ounces) condensed
   Cheddar cheese soup
½ cup sour cream
¼ cup milk
½ teaspoon seasoned salt
1 bag (16 ounces) frozen
   vegetable combination
   (broccoli, corn, red pepper),
   thawed and drained

1 bag (16 ounces) frozen
   vegetable combination
   (brussels sprouts, carrots,
   cauliflower), thawed and
   drained
1 cup (4 ounces) shredded
   Cheddar cheese
1 can (2.8 ounces) Durkee
   French Fried Onions

(continued)

Saucy Garden Patch Vegetables

Preheat oven to 375°. In large bowl, combine soup, sour cream, milk, seasoned salt, vegetables, *½ cup* cheese and *½ can* French Fried Onions. Spoon into 8×12-inch baking dish. Bake, covered, at 375° for 40 minutes or until vegetables are done. Top with remaining cheese and onions; bake, uncovered, 3 minutes or until onions are golden brown.   *Makes 8 to 10 servings*

MICROWAVE DIRECTIONS: Prepare vegetable mixture as above; spoon into 8×12-inch microwave-safe dish. Cook, covered, on HIGH 10 to 12 minutes or until vegetables are done. Stir vegetables halfway through cooking time. Top with remaining cheese and onions; cook, uncovered, 1 minute or until cheese melts. Let stand 5 minutes.

ZUCCHINI PAISANO

Ready to bake in just 10 easy minutes

3 tablespoons vegetable oil
3 small zucchini, thinly sliced
  (about 3 cups)
2 cups sliced mushrooms
1 can (15 ounces) tomato sauce
  or tomato bits in tomato
  puree
¾ teaspoon dried basil,
  crumbled

⅛ teaspoon garlic powder
1 can (2.8 ounces) Durkee
  French Fried Onions
½ cup ricotta cheese
⅓ cup (about 1½ ounces) grated
  Parmesan cheese
¼ cup milk
1 egg, slightly beaten

Preheat oven to 375°. In large skillet, heat oil. Cook zucchini and mushrooms in oil until zucchini is tender-crisp, about 5 minutes; remove from heat. Stir in tomato sauce, seasonings and ½ *can* French Fried Onions. Pour into greased 1½-quart casserole. In small bowl, combine ricotta and Parmesan cheeses, milk and egg; blend until smooth. Spread cheese mixture over surface of vegetables. Bake, uncovered, at 375° for 30 minutes or until cheese topping is set. Top with remaining onions; bake, uncovered, 3 minutes or until onions are golden brown. *Makes 4 to 6 servings*

FESTIVE SWEET POTATO COMBO

Ready to bake in just 7 easy minutes

1 can (40 ounces) sweet
  potatoes, drained
1 can (2.8 ounces) Durkee
  French Fried Onions
1 medium apple, sliced into
  thin wedges
1 can (8 ounces) crushed
  pineapple, undrained

3 tablespoons packed brown
  sugar
2 tablespoons butter or
  margarine, melted
1 teaspoon ground cinnamon

Preheat oven to 375°. In 8×12-inch baking dish, layer sweet potatoes, ½ *can* French Fried Onions and the apple. In small bowl, thoroughly combine pineapple, brown sugar, butter and cinnamon; pour pineapple mixture over sweet potato mixture. Bake, covered, at 375° for 30 minutes or until heated through. Top with remaining onions; bake, uncovered, 3 minutes or until onions are golden brown. *Makes 4 to 6 servings*

THREE-CHEESE MACARONI

Ready to bake in just 12 easy minutes

3 cups macaroni, cooked in
   unsalted water and
   drained
1 can (11 ounces) condensed
   Cheddar cheese soup
1 cup milk
½ teaspoon ground mustard
¼ teaspoon seasoned salt
   (optional)
¼ teaspoon pepper

½ cup (2 ounces) shredded
   Swiss cheese
½ cup (2 ounces) shredded
   Cheddar cheese
½ cup (2 ounces) grated
   Parmesan cheese
1 can (2.8 ounces) Durkee
   French Fried Onions

Preheat oven to 350°. In 1½-quart casserole, combine hot macaroni,
soup, milk, seasonings, *¼ cup each* of Swiss, Cheddar and Parmesan
cheese and *½ can* French Fried Onions. Bake, covered, at 350° for 25
minutes or until heated through. Top with remaining cheeses and
onions; bake, uncovered, 5 minutes or until onions are golden
brown.   *Makes 4 to 6 main-dish servings*

MICROWAVE DIRECTIONS: In 1½-quart microwave-safe casserole,
prepare macaroni mixture as above. Cook, covered, on HIGH 10 to
11 minutes or until heated through. Stir casserole halfway through
cooking time. Top with remaining cheeses and onions; cook,
uncovered, 1 minute or until cheeses melt. Let stand 5 minutes.

COUNTRY CORN BAKE

Ready to bake in just 5 easy minutes

5 slices bacon, fried crisp
1 bag (20 ounces) frozen whole
   kernel corn, thawed and
   drained
1 can (10¾ ounces) condensed
   cream of potato soup
½ cup milk
½ cup thinly sliced celery

1 tablespoon diced pimiento
   (optional)
½ teaspoon seasoned salt
½ cup (2 ounces) shredded
   Cheddar cheese
1 can (2.8 ounces) Durkee
   French Fried Onions

Preheat oven to 375°. In large bowl, combine corn, soup, milk,
celery, pimiento, seasoned salt, *¼ cup* cheese and *½ can* French
Fried Onions. Crumble 3 slices bacon; stir into corn mixture. Spoon
corn mixture into 8-inch square baking dish. Bake, covered, at 375°
for 40 to 45 minutes or until hot and bubbly. Top with remaining
bacon slices, cheese and onions; bake, uncovered, 3 minutes or until
onions are golden brown.   *Makes 4 to 6 servings*

ARTICHOKE 'N BROCCOLI FANFARE

Ready to bake in just 10 easy minutes

1 package (10 ounces) frozen chopped broccoli, thawed and drained
1 cup (4 ounces) shredded Swiss cheese
1 can (2.8 ounces) Durkee French Fried Onions
1 egg
1 can (10¾ ounces) condensed cream of celery soup
¼ cup milk
2 tablespoons white wine (optional)
½ teaspoon dried marjoram, crumbled
1 can (8½ ounces) artichoke hearts, rinsed, drained and cut into halves

Preheat oven to 350°. In small bowl, combine broccoli, ½ cup cheese, ½ *can* French Fried Onions and the egg. Stir until well blended; set aside. In medium bowl, combine soup, milk, wine and marjoram. Stir *half* the soup mixture into broccoli mixture; pour into 1-quart oval or round baking dish. Stand artichoke halves in broccoli mixture with cut sides against side of dish. Pour remaining soup mixture over artichokes and broccoli. Bake, covered, at 350° for 30 minutes or until heated through. Top with remaining cheese and onions; bake, uncovered, 5 minutes or until onions are golden brown.   *Makes 4 to 6 servings*

MICROWAVE DIRECTIONS: Prepare broccoli and soup mixtures as above. In 1-quart round microwave-safe dish, assemble casserole as above. Cook, covered, on HIGH 10 to 12 minutes or until heated through. Stir broccoli mixture halfway through cooking time. Top with remaining cheese and onions; cook, uncovered, 1 minute or until cheese melts. Let stand 5 minutes.

ZESTY ONION FRITTATA

Ready to bake in just 8 easy minutes

1 can (8¾ ounces) whole kernel corn, drained
1 can (4 ounces) chopped green chilies, drained
5 eggs, slightly beaten
½ cup sour cream
¼ cup all-purpose flour
½ teaspoon chili powder
¼ teaspoon seasoned salt
1 cup (4 ounces) shredded Cheddar cheese
1 jar (12 ounces) mild or medium picante sauce
1 can (2.8 ounces) Durkee French Fried Onions

(continued)

Zesty Onion Frittata

Preheat oven to 350°. In medium bowl, combine corn, chilies, eggs, sour cream, flour, seasonings, *½ cup* cheese, *¼ cup* picante sauce and *½ can* French Fried Onions. Pour into greased 10-inch round baking dish. Bake, covered, at 350° for 35 minutes or until knife inserted in center comes out clean. Pour remaining picante sauce around edge of dish. Top sauce with remaining cheese and onions; bake, uncovered, 5 minutes or until onions are golden brown. Garnish as desired. *Makes 4 to 6 servings*

MICROWAVE DIRECTIONS: Prepare corn mixture as above; pour into 10-inch round microwave-safe dish. Cook, loosely covered, on HIGH 10 to 12 minutes or until knife inserted in center comes out clean. Stir corn mixture halfway through cooking time. Top with remaining picante sauce, cheese and onions as above; cook, uncovered, 2 minutes or until cheese melts. Let stand 5 minutes.

TANGY BLUE CHEESE VEGETABLES

Ready to bake in just 10 easy minutes

1 package (3 ounces) cream
  cheese, softened
¼ cup (2 ounces) crumbled blue
  cheese
¾ cup milk
1 jar (4½ ounces) whole
  mushrooms, drained

1 bag (16 ounces) frozen
  vegetable combination
  (peas, carrots, cauliflower),
  thawed and drained
1 can (2.8 ounces) Durkee
  French Fried Onions

Preheat oven to 375°. In medium saucepan, combine cream cheese, blue cheese and milk. Cook and stir over medium heat until smooth. Stir in mushrooms, vegetables and ½ *can* French Fried Onions; pour into 1-quart casserole. Bake, covered, at 375° for 30 minutes or until vegetables are done. Top with remaining onions; bake, uncovered, 3 minutes or until onions are golden brown.

Makes 4 to 6 servings

MICROWAVE DIRECTIONS: In 1-quart microwave-safe casserole, combine cream cheese, blue cheese and milk. Cook, covered, on HIGH 5 to 6 minutes or until cheeses melt, stirring mixture halfway through cooking time. Add mushrooms, vegetables and ½ *can* onions; cook, covered, 5 to 7 minutes or until vegetables are done. Stir halfway through cooking time. Top with remaining onions; cook, uncovered, 1 minute. Let stand 5 minutes.

CRUNCHY SCALLOPED CELERY

Ready to bake in just 10 easy minutes

3 cups diagonally sliced celery
1 package (10 ounces) frozen
  peas, thawed and drained
1 can (8 ounces) sliced water
  chestnuts, drained
1 can (4 ounces) mushroom
  stems and pieces, drained

1 can (10¾ ounces) condensed
  cream of celery soup
¼ cup milk
½ teaspoon seasoned salt
1 can (2.8 ounces) Durkee
  French Fried Onions

Preheat oven to 350°. In large saucepan, simmer celery in small amount of boiling water until tender-crisp, about 5 minutes; drain. Stir in peas, water chestnuts, mushrooms, soup, milk, seasoned salt and ½ *can* French Fried Onions. Pour into 1½-quart casserole. Bake, uncovered, at 350° for 20 minutes or until heated through. Top with remaining onions; bake, uncovered, 5 minutes or until onions are golden brown.

Makes 4 to 6 servings

RANCH-STYLE EGGS

Ready to bake in just 5 easy minutes

1 can (14½ ounces) whole
    tomatoes, undrained and
    cut up
1 can (8 ounces) tomato sauce
¼ teaspoon garlic powder

1 can (2.8 ounces) Durkee
    French Fried Onions
6 eggs
½ cup (2 ounces) shredded
    Cheddar cheese
6 (6-inch) corn or flour tortillas
Shredded lettuce

Preheat oven to 400°. In 8×12-inch baking dish, combine tomatoes, tomato sauce, garlic powder and ½ *can* French Fried Onions; stir to blend. Break eggs into tomato mixture, spacing evenly. Bake, uncovered, at 400° for 15 to 20 minutes or until eggs are cooked to desired doneness. Top eggs with cheese and remaining onions; bake, uncovered, 1 to 3 minutes or until onions are golden brown. Serve on tortillas topped with shredded lettuce. *Makes 6 servings*

CROWD-PLEASING VEGETABLE PILAF

Ready to bake in just 15 easy minutes

3 cups cooked unsalted regular
    rice (1 cup uncooked)
1 can (10¾ ounces) condensed
    cream of mushroom soup
1 can (10¾ ounces) condensed
    cream of celery soup
1 cup (4 ounces) shredded
    Cheddar cheese
1 jar (2 ounces) diced
    pimiento, drained

1 package (10 ounces) frozen
    chopped spinach, thawed
    and well drained
1 package (10 ounces) frozen
    chopped broccoli, thawed
    and drained
1 can (2.8 ounces) Durkee
    French Fried Onions

Preheat oven to 350°. To hot rice in saucepan, add soups, cheese and pimiento; stir well and set aside. In medium bowl, combine spinach, broccoli and ½ *can* French Fried Onions. Spread *half* the rice mixture in 8×12-inch baking dish; top with vegetable mixture, then with remaining rice mixture. Bake, covered, at 350° for 40 minutes or until heated through. Top with remaining onions; bake, uncovered, 5 minutes or until onions are golden brown.

Makes 8 to 10 servings

MICROWAVE DIRECTIONS: Prepare rice and vegetable mixtures and layer as above in 8×12-inch microwave-safe dish. Cook, covered, on HIGH 12 to 14 minutes or until heated through. Rotate dish halfway through cooking time. Top with remaining onions; cook, uncovered, 1 minute. Let stand 5 minutes.

INDEX